THE TRICKS OF
FINANCIAL
TERRORISTS:

An Exposé about the 419 Phenomenon in Nigeria

Raymond Rotimi Akinfolarin

ISBN: 146111716X
ISBN-13: 9781461117162
Library of Congress Control Number: 2011912564
CreateSpace, North Charleston, SC

Foreword

Many supposedly enlightened and intelligent people have fallen victim to the scourge of fraudsters in Nigeria during the past two decades. Despite different headlines, given by both the print and electronic media to this rampaging activity, there have been few attempts aimed at inoculating potential victims. In the book, The Tricks of Financial Terrorists has come at last, an ingenious effort to provide a compendium of the intrigues usually employed by criminally minded individuals or gangs, to deprive innocent, gullible and unsuspecting victims of their finances and other valuables. The scope of intrigues is quite elaborate extending from street cards' games, money doubling, making of fake currency through chemical wash, palm reading, fortune telling, purchase and sale of bogus products and Local Purchase Order to sale and rent of real estate, use of other people's property as loan security, employment, school and visa scams, over-invoicing trap, thrift fraud (The Wonder Bank), petroleum products scam, foreign exchange scam, stock market fraud, Internet fraud, unregistered NGO's soliciting foreign Grants, unsolicited payment for contract, false Will and foreign donations bait, etc.

The Tricks of Financial Terrorists serves a dual purpose of providing knowledge and insight into what has become a major challenge to the national image of Nigeria, thereby making people to become more alert and less vulnerable while, equally sending a signal to those involved in this criminal act that their days are numbered. For too long in this country, people have capitalized on the ignorance of their fellow citizens and foreign nationals, to dispossess them of huge amounts of money and other valuable assets. The trauma upon their victims, arising from such financial crimes can only be imagined, given the problem of inadequate reporting of these incidents.

While acknowledging that all manners of tricks employed in financial crimes may not be exhaustive in one compilation, due credit must be given to the author of the book for a very extensive treatment of the subject. This book certainly has its social security significance as much as a foreign relations and investment promotion perspectives. It touches also on the psychological as to why people behave as they do, why some people are more prone to being victims than others and why some engage in criminal acts of financial deception, while others seek socially acceptable ways of reaching the top, under the same circumstance.

Written in simple style and progressively from minor street tricks to the most absurd, it is an all comers book meant for every home; it provides information of immense benefits to children and adults. Parents would not regret having the contents of this book introduced to their wards; if for nothing else, it holds the promise of saving parents from being told one day, that Junior's school fees have been lost to a fraudster. Most significantly, I would recommend the book for the school system and all institutions of government that have a stake in building a positive image for Nigeria.

Ijide Wilson PhD

Acknowledgement

To God Almighty is the Glory. All thanks and praises to the Father through whose guidance and protection I was able to complete the research and production of this book, put together particularly in the interest of my beloved country, **Nigeria** and for the benefit of Mankind in general.

My appreciation goes to Colonel. **Wilson Ijide** PhD, who out of his military tight schedule, created time to write the foreword.
I appreciate the good job, encouragement and patience of Mr. `**Dipo Onabanjo** who read the manuscript and made necessary amendments.

I seize this opportunity to express my gratitude to the entire board, management, and staff of Createspace.com especially Project Team 2.

I thank my entire family especially Mrs. **Abimbola Adewole-Oshikoya** and friends for their moral support.

My special appreciation goes to my bosom friend Mr. **Richard Adenikinju** for his friendship loyalty and unquantifiable support towards the success of the book.

It was one long year of research work, and I thank those who for obvious reasons chose to remain anonymous but made the research successful by providing me with the much needed assistance during my point-to-point search for materials.

Finally, the book of Proverbs chapter 20, verse 17 says: "Bread of deceit is sweet to a man; but afterward his mouth shall be filled with gravel" (KJV).

My prayer for every reader is never to experience the destructive tricks of financial terrorists masquerading as do-gooders in today's complex world.

Thank you all.

Contents

PART TWO

Introduction

The famous Section 419 of the Nigerian penal code was designed to punish fraudsters who take money or other valuables from person(s), corporate bodies, or governments under false pretenses. The law was revised and expanded under Decree Number 13 and entitled "Advance Fee Fraud and Other Fraud Offenses Decree 1995"; this was repealed in 2005 after the inception of democratic rule. The 2005 act was then amended in 2006 and entitled "Advance Fee Fraud and Other Fraud Related Offences Act, 2006."* This act is certainly not new in Nigeria, whose penal codes took their inspiration from Britain, its colonial master. But the "419" law is not peculiar to Nigeria and Britain. It exists all over the world in varying degrees and under different legal codes.

However, it is the frequency with which a law must be appealed to that determines a nation's notoriety for a crime. Nigeria is no doubt notorious for crime because of its higher rate of occurrence in the country compared with other countries of the world. Virtually every household knows what the phrase "419"—pronounced "four-one-nine"—means in the Nigerian parlance, such that children below the age of five use it as a derogatory remark (even though they do not really appreciate its true meaning).

But why would anybody obtain things under false pretences? In today's world, greed is overcoming the better part of man. The desire to build up mountains of wealth legally acquired or not has made many people to engage in fraudulence. Our culture of celebrating wealth does not help matters, either, because it causes many people to believe that the end justifies the means. Well-known "419" kingpins are being awarded chieftaincy titles, and they enjoy opulent lives at the expense of their poor victims. In some cases, they even create false titles and appellations for themselves at the early stages—when they are not yet successful enough to buy titles—in order to shore up their images and build up some credibility for themselves. In the

Nigerian milieu, examples of such titles include *otunba*, chief, deacon, pastor, *alhaji*, doctor, prince, etc.

It is a pity that our society relegates genuine success to the background while celebrating thieves and vagabonds who make it to the tops of their various illegal careers. Rebranding Nigeria without taming the monstrous "419" may end up an image-laundering façade. It is the collective attitudes of individual citizens—not slogans—that reflect the entire country's image both home and abroad. It is all about the people. Again, it is not what you claim to be but rather others' perceptions of you that earn you your deserved ranking.

The "419" plague does not only affect a country's image: it gnaws at the economy, too, rendering all economic policies ineffectual and throwing many into the poverty trap.

It should be conceded that, generally, fraudsters are grandmasters in their chosen "professions." Their ingenuity is almost incomparable. No doubt, it takes some brain to design and perpetrate frauds. But the irony of it all is that had such efforts been positively applied to the economy and other useful purposes, they still would have been the millionaires they now are and perhaps profited even more, while the society would have also reaped some benefits.

A good number of 419 kingpins choose the noble law profession but only for the purpose of twisting and swinging the law to their side by duping their undiscerning victims. Others obtain a degree in criminology with the intention of learning what they need to know to establish a local organized crime network and nurture it into a global criminal empire with branches across continents.

It is some people's belief that fraudsters' activities are being spiritually enhanced in view of the enigmatic circumstances surrounding their operations. While such a school of thought could not be totally discarded, victims' greed and gullibility are largely responsible for their woes, and these two major factors cut across race and gender lines.

The prime aim of this exposition is to let the entire world know that the majority of Nigerians are good people, while only the very few unpatriotic elements amongst them are responsible for the country's

uncomplimentary global image. Again, and perhaps more importantly, there is the urgent need to attack and destroy this cankerworm
by exposing the fraudsters' tricks to the world, thereby reducing their
patrons both home and abroad to the barest minimum. In this way, it
is expected that the perpetrators of this dangerous crime will change
their line of business to more meaningful trades that would be of mutual benefit to themselves and the global community at large.

PART ONE
LOCAL LEVEL

CHAPTER ONE

Street Cards Game

Cards game is a popular relaxation game usually played by two or more persons. It is also played for financial gain when money is put at stake, but this is only allowed at licensed houses like hotel casinos.

However, street cards game, as it is called, is illegal street gambling operated by fraudsters to deceive greedy bystanders. Growing up, I learned about street cards game, which was commonly played between the sixties and the eighties.

In street cards game, there are usually three different cards at the disposal of the promoter. He displays them, showing which one of the three cards wins the prize at stake. Afterward, he lays the cards face-down so that the unsuspecting victim can have the chance to pick the winning card out of the three. The winning prize is always double what the client stakes so as to make the game attractive to greedy passersby and onlookers.

One common way in which this trick is performed is for a member of the fraudster's gang to stand in the crowd. He is allowed to win the game over and over until the promoter, acting annoyed, bars him from staking anymore money. Playing along, he leaves the venue only to sneak back and attract the attention of one of the onlookers, to whom he then pretends to divulge the secret of his winning technique. Anyone who gives him audience and plays the game as he advises will surely fall prey and lose money because he has been deceived!

If the hoodwinked player fails to pick the winning card during his first attempt—which is always the case—the "ex-champion" blames him as if it were his own personal money that had been staked and lost. Unaware of the deceit, however, and propelled by the greed for money, the foolish player continues to stake his money until he empties his pockets.

Another way in which this trick is performed is to actually allow someone to win at first and then order him to leave; this makes the game look real and impartial. Then, someone else out of the crowd—this one, unknown to others, is a member of the fraudster's gang—will step out to stake money, and he will deliberately lose two or more rounds. Afterward he will appear to be on top of the game and start winning like his other barred colleague. It is all make-believe, though, because the new champion is also part of the scam, and before long, he will also be barred.

It is this person who will now convince the doubting Thomases in the crowd by calling some people aside and pretending to disclose the tricks of the game to them. Remember that he lost a few rounds when he stepped in, after which he appeared to master the tricks and become a threat to the promoter's business by winning until he was stopped. So, it is this winning experience of his that he will be sharing with others who have unwittingly fallen into his trap.

One's vulnerability and susceptibility to "419" scam is always a good barometer to measure one's greed, although there are some exceptional cases. I have witnessed children sent on errands by their parents or guardians losing such errands' money to the tricksters. You only get to know the value of the purposes for which such money was meant when they break down crying like babies and begging for money to replace what they have lost through greed.

Housewives fall prey to the tricksters, too, losing their families' food allowances to these street boys. Greed has no gender and no respect for one's socioeconomic status. Whoever cannot tame his or her greed instinct will be a victim.

If you do not belong to the gang, there is no way you can win. It does not matter how smart you are: they are always ahead of you because it is a career they have chosen, and you cannot beat them to it. Students who want to get rich quick stake their school fees in small proportions until they lose all. If such students happen to come from poor homes, the result may be an unfortunate change of destiny.

Guarding against falling prey is easy. Whoever is not disciplined enough to see such games as sheer amusement should stay out of street crowd shows.

Most people are gullible when it comes to get-rich-quick propositions. Those street boys may shift their operations from one street to the next, yet they will always find people to deceive and swindle. Even when people see others crying because they were cheated, they believe it could not happen to them—but at the end of the day, they become fatal victims of their individual greed and indiscretion.

Another reason one might fall prey is because one is somewhere one is not supposed to be. For example, street gambling is outlawed, so nobody can legally or morally justify engaging in a street cards game or even being a part of the crowd watching the game: it's all illegal. Children in particular should be discouraged from watching and participating in gambling. They should instead be taught about the beauty of having a legitimate means of livelihood and contentment.

CHAPTER TWO

Money-Doubling

Money-doubling is investment fraudulent trick that presents itself as legitimate investment. The investor gives x amount of money to a "doubler" in expectation of receiving twice x back within a period of time as short as twenty-four hours.

Legitimate investment is the key to clean wealth. Farmers invest in their farms by planting and nurturing their crops. Placing money in a fixed account with a bank is an investment, and buying into the shares of publicly quoted companies is another way of investing. Traders invest by buying their goods for y amount of money and then moving the goods to another point and selling them at y amount plus x, where x covers overheads and profit.

There are millions of legitimate investments, but money-doubling surely is not one because it defies all investment theories. All investments have their own waiting or incubating period, but a twenty-four-hour turnaround time for a 100 percent return is simply impossible.

Money-doublers have several ways of presenting the illicit proposal to their greedy patrons, and this chapter will deal with the most common two of them. The first one is when a close friend or associate of a would-be victim, having knowledge his friend's financial status, talks him into how to make a 100 percent return on his money within just one day. In 419 parlance, the marketer here is called the catcher (trickster) and the victim-to-be is referred to as the *mugu* (fool). The catcher intends to "catch," or lure, his friend, the *mugu*—Nigerian slang for "fool"—into a trap.

The catcher cajoles the *mugu* to come to his base, where the striker—the boss who calls the shots—is waiting. Now the catcher has caught a *mugu* for the striker to strike. The catcher now convinces the striker of his closeness to the *mugu*, thereby giving the striker confidence that the *mugu* is not flippant and can maintain secrecy. Having done that, the catcher withdraws, and the real game commences. The *mugu* will then be administered an oath of secrecy along with the striker by a make-believe native doctor who is also part of the scam.

Some of the components of the oath-taking materials include the blood of both the *mugu* and the striker, which is obtained through minor incisions on both of them and then drained into a waiting cup of dry gin or schnapps. The fake native doctor goes on to perform the rituals, during which the *mugu* is made to know that the day he divulges whatever he experiences during their transaction to a third party is the day he dies. Both parties then share a part of a kola nut and drink the blood concoction.

To convince the *mugu* that getting rich is not a tea party, the striker takes the victim to a shrine—another make-believe element of the scam—either within or outside their base of operation. It is at this shrine that an idol or spirit prescribes what the *mugu* needs for his prayers to be answered and explains that these things will not come cheap. This is where the grand extortion begins.

The spirits clumsily demand that the *mugu* must be told the costs of those items that will enable him to advance such money to the striker who will help him procure them. The idea of money-doubling is sold to the *mugu* by the catcher as a twenty-four-hour process, but it is also explained to him that he could be placed on a daily adjournment for over a period of one month, depending on his financial capability. He pays for one expensive item or another on every appointed date to facilitate his financial breakthrough.

The fact that he has already been deceived to swear to a make-believe oath—thereby creating a fear of death in his mind—coupled with the fact that he continues to part with more and more money as the scam goes on, the *mugu* never rethinks in the middle of the game and never considers withdrawing to minimize his loss; rather, he continues to be driven by the power of greed and, choosing not to lose the amount he has already invested, he puts in a little more effort to arrive home and dry with double the amount he initially invested. This "little effort" leads many a victim into huge debts and even sometimes brings them to sell real estate property to conclude a deal that never existed in the first place.

This scam sometimes leads to suicide on the parts of the victims, who eventually lose almost everything of value to the fraudsters. In most cases, what leads the victims to commit suicide is that they are constrained from sharing their pains with their loved ones—including their spouses—for fear of sudden death resulting from the breach of the oath of secrecy they've sworn to.

The close associates of victims will only notice sudden changes in their attitudes, including but not limited to the loss of appetite as a result of thinking and withdrawal syndrome. In order to not share his experience with others, including family members, a victim always withdraws to himself, even at home. He sometimes stays in the bedroom, either spending his time thinking of a way out of this huge debt crisis that has been occasioned by his having been duped or contemplating suicide, depending on the extent of damage and the victim's capacity to absorb shock.

Despite the damage suffered by the victims, the scam always ends in a win-win situation for the fraudsters because they always succeed in reaping from where they did not sow, and the deceptive oath effectively restrains their victims from taking legal actions against them.

The catcher's second approach to the money-doubling scam is to casually ask a stranger for directions to a popular location or street that anyone living in the area would be able to easily locate and describe. In most cases, the catcher has some vital information about the victim before he approaches him, but once his victim cooperates with him, he promises to bless him for rendering such assistance. The catcher also poses as a powerful spiritualist who can help someone out of whatever type of unpalatable life situation he finds himself. Since every living being has his or her own challenges at any given time, a stranger revealing what one has been going through in the last five to ten years becomes credible.

The next step is for the catcher to fix an appointment with the *mugu* at his operational base. The victim is typically so eager that he laments that the appointed date is too far for him, but then the catcher tells him that it is the appointed day of the spirits and not that of man. The victim is then sternly warned against sharing his experience in this regard with anyone. That is always the rule because if he tells someone who already knows their tricks, the deal will be foiled.

When the victim gets there on the appointed day and is ushered in, the catcher and the striker continue to reveal certain things about his life. Stunned by such revelations, the victim will, in apparent anxiety, ask them what to do either to get rich quick or to get out of the problems facing him.

If the victim is a woman, the catcher and the striker will say that it is either barrenness or a lack of a suitor that is causing her problems, but whichever card they place on the table, they are acting on information obtained about the victim from a close relation and hence the victim becomes enslaved to them.

They thereafter propose a spiritual cleansing bath that could involve ritual births or the killing of animals such as rams or goats. At the venue of the cleansing bath, they apply water to a sponge and soap and rub it against the victim's head, to his chagrin, and a sudden deafening explosion then issues from the sponge, causing the victim's hair to be burnt. This is meant to appear to confirm what has been told about the victim's numerous enemies, who do not want him to progress in life and are hell-bent to change his destiny for the worse. The explosion, however, is contrived. It is just a simple chemical reaction of black soap, gunpowder, carbide, and water. Gunpowder is an explosive, and carbide's reaction to water triggers the gunpowder's explosion. All the chemicals are cleverly inserted in the sponge that is used to wash the victim's head.

But because the fraudsters pretend to interpret the explosion as a spiritual warning that they should not go ahead with the cleansing, the victim is forced to go on his knees and beg and promise almost everything he has if only they will go ahead and conclude the cleansing process so as to set him free from spiritual bondage. After much appeal and promises, the fraudsters then raise their charges and make unimaginable demands. They are at this point working within a particular net worth framework obtained from a close associate of the victim—their informant and a cobeneficiary of the scam. In short, they demand from him more or less almost everything he has.

After draining the victim of all his property and money, his condition of course becomes worse than it was when they met him, but he is again restrained from sharing his experience and losses as this would amount to breaching the oath he swore to at the beginning of the deceitful exercise. This is another version of a fraud in which the weaknesses of the victim and threats to his survival are exploited for monetary gains. The lesson here is to ignore any transaction or deal that demands absolute secrecy or nondisclosure to a third party. Such a deal is certainly illegal, and in most cases, it ends in disaster. Do not get involved. You have been warned!

CHAPTER THREE

Money-Minting Through Chemical Wash

One of a nation's statutory functions is to print its currency either by itself or through a third-party corporate body contracted for the purpose. A country's currency is its legal tender and means of exchange. Governments regulate the amount of currency printed and released into circulation at all times so as to maintain the value of the money and prevent—or at least control—the level of inflation.

Money-minting is one of the most common tricks used by fraudsters to swindle their greedy victims. The victims are so gullible that they fail to question the rationale behind why someone would show them such an easy way to huge wealth. Experience has shown that, in most cases, the victims are taken in by the cleverness of their fraudulent assailants.

Typically, a fraudster approaches his victim, who is usually a successful professional or businessperson—a caterer, for example. The fraudster might approach a caterer in her restaurant and invite her to meet his boss, who is preparing a grand wedding for his child in his residence.

Upon arriving there, the fraudster will usher in the caterer and begin negotiating with her. In the middle of such a negotiation, a young man will suddenly stroll in to ask the boss to do him some favor, but the boss will ignore him, preferring to give more attention to the business deal with the caterer. The young man will continue to put pressure on the boss, who will pretend to lose his self-control and appear to attempt to physically attack the former. Uncomfortable with the situation, the caterer will ask what the matter is all about. The boss will point to three or four trunk boxes in a corner of the room and explain how he, as a customs officer, helped the young man to clear them at the airport. He will say the boxes contain assorted wristwatches and that they were impounded following the young man's inability to pay appropriate customs duty but that he bailed out the latter by paying the duty on his behalf. He will insist that he will only release the boxes once the boy has paid back his money, and he will say that, after all, the boxes only contain mere carbon papers cut into small sizes, contrary to the boy's earlier declaration of wristwatches. On hearing that, the caterer will request to see the contents of the boxes. The boy will then open them up and tell the caterer in a whisper that the boxes contain money in a raw form that needs some chemicals to develop into real money. Inside one of the boxes will be a tiny bottle containing some liquid, and the boy will ask for a small bowl of water. He will put some detergent, the liquid, and some carefully selected carbon-like papers from one of the boxes into the bowl.

After stirring the mixture by hand for about thirty seconds, to the apparent surprise of everybody in the room, the paper cuttings will begin to lose their dark color and then change into different denominations of United States dollars. With self-satisfaction, the boy will now hand over the wet notes to the boss, while assuring him that they are just samples of the full contents of the boxes. He will, however, stress the need to source for some five hundred thousand naira or more to wash the contents of all the boxes, which, put together, come out to five hundred million U.S. dollars.

At this point, the boy will insist that the three—including the caterer, who by now has been taken in by what she has seen—swear to an oath of secrecy as they agree to convert the pieces of paper to millions of dollars. The logic is that an oath of secrecy is required between three "new friends" who have just discovered a treasure trove and cannot brook any betrayal from any quarters. As is usual in this part of the world, the oath involves using the blood of those involved in the deal. The operation is simple: a small quantity of blood is obtained from each participant, the blood is mixed with a cup of dry gin, and the mixture—taken with kola nut—is jointly shared.

Having done this to secure the sealed lips and cooperation of the caterer, the boss divides the content of the boxes equally between the trio and levies each party its share of the naira cost of washing the raw dollars. The total cost is 166,666 naira, which is to be invested for a return of 166,666,666 United States dollars. Off her guard, the caterer has forgotten about her initial mission of prospecting for a catering contract. She is now obsessed with how she could bite into the unfolding deal and become a multimillionaire in hard currency!

The striker will then call the *mugu* aside and give her the washed dollars to change to naira on her way home so that she can discover whether the money is genuine or not.

Before long, she will be back. She will have successfully changed the washed dollars to naira, and so she will have brought with her her share of the cost of chemical to wash the rest of the money. And just then, the owner of the boxes will cede his share of the dollars to any of the other two ready to raise money to buy chemical to wash his share of the dollar bills.

Greed is the name of the game. Once the caterer falls for the first proposal, she is then good "meat" for the second offer, which is even more attractive. With her eyes on two-thirds of the whole deal, she moves fast to raise more money. Having secured almost three hundred million dollars by her calculated expectations, the boy will collect her cash in naira and pretend to look for the chemical, spending about two days stalling for more time. Meanwhile, madam multibillionaire-to-be will be preoccupied with dreams of how she will spend the expected windfall.

After those two days, the errant partner in crime will arrive late to the venue of their meeting. As he enters the room, he will stumble, and the bottle containing the golden chemical will drop to the ground and explode! The caterer will then ask herself what she should do: forget about the deal or start all over? To simply forget about the deal would amount to losing everything, which couldn't possible appeal to the greedy victim, so she has to follow through and begin to raise money for the chemical again. When she cannot raise the needed cash, she will then begin to sell her property at heavily discounted rates.

When enough money has been raised and the boy brings a new bottle of the chemical, he will drop it off with the striker, who in turn will keep it in a refrigerator. As soon as the boy and the *mugu* demand it, it is brought out of the fridge and explodes again; the reason the boy will give this time is that it was not supposed to be refrigerated in the first place. So, the blame goes to the striker. Undaunted and prompted by the allure of money, the *mugu* will insist that the deal must be concluded. If there is no more property left to be sold, then she will borrow!

The extortion goes on and on like this because there is no end to the occurrence of one hitch or another during the washing process. If the price of the chemical does not shoot up astronomically from the very limited source, the striker may report that the owner of the boxes who usually goes to buy the chemical has absconded. Then, to bring the game to a close, a fake policeman will burst in, and the victim will be made to bribe her way out of the problem! This extortion is always ended with a fake law enforcement agent.

Let's consider for a moment what they put together to come up with the minting scam package. The black papers cut into currency size are carbon papers spread on top of loads of old newspapers that actually constitute 98 percent of the content of the boxes. The few dollars washed are initially soaked in an iodine solution, which causes them to appear dark brown or black, and the chemical used to wash them—which has a reaction with the iodine in soap water—simply bleaches off the iodine color. The only real money in all the boxes is just the three currency notes that are washed and changed into naira.

Generally, it takes two to tango. The scammers are known criminals, and the *mugus* are in most cases innocent. Such victims are often propelled by greed, however, and thus cannot but be adjudged guilty along with the perpetrators. The lesson, therefore, is that one should not be carried away by mouthwatering business propositions. Remember, if it sounds too good to be true, it is certainly untrue!

CHAPTER FOUR

Palm-Reading

Palm-reading dates back to man's earliest existence. People consult genuine palm-readers for many reasons, ranging from considerations of health to wealth. Palm-reading scam victims are some of the very few who are actually innocent and whose interest is not entirely greed-driven. They are mostly victims of hypnotism and may not be referred to as *mugus*.

The scammers sometimes approach their victims on the street but more often in a taxicab. The taxicab scenario is what I am going to describe.

Usually, the operational cab will contain three gentle-looking men, that is, the driver, a passenger in the front seat, and a passenger in the back seat. Their victim will join the man in the back seat, and an introduction to the effect that the two passengers are foreign spiritualists will take place. They will go further to say they are in the country to pray for motherless babies in a variety of motherless homes around the country. Once the victim allows them to pray for her, she gets hypnotized, and they take all she has.

This is how the real hypnotism starts. After their short prayer, they ask their victim (usually a woman) to spit on her palm, after which she will be asked to turn the palm upside down so that the spit will appear on the back of her hand. From that moment on, she is their puppet, and she will be doing their bidding as long as they wish her to. They may decide to take her to a secluded area of the city to extract information about what she has and where it is. If she lives alone, she will lead them to her house, where she will give them all her light and movable valuables in such a way that neighbors' suspicions will not be raised. They will lead her to a bank to withdraw all her life savings while they wait outside in the cab. After handing over her money to the fraudsters, the victim will still ride in the same cab with them to wherever they wish because she is completely under their spell.

There are instances when the fraudsters feel they do not get enough from the victim over the course of the day, and they will ask her to go and borrow money from her friends or to get a loan from the office and bring it to them at an appointed place and time the following day. The sorry aspect of this type of scam is that the very moment the victim is released, she comes back to her senses and starts wondering what really happened to her, but unfortunately, it is always too late because the fraudsters will have been long gone.

This is one of the very few instances in which the victims are not those who want to get rich quick by cutting corners. The message here, instead, is that you should not board a cab already occupied by passengers, especially if you are a woman.

CHAPTER FIVE

Fortune-Telling

Fortune-telling is similar to palm-reading. They both deal with one's life past, present, and future: they tell us how to avert dangers, remove encumbrances to prosperity, and improve personal health. Fake fortune-tellers capitalize on the gullibility of people with peculiar problems who are desperately looking for solutions at any cost. The fraudsters in this case get their victims' data through close associates of the victims. Below is a true story of a fortune-telling scam.

Once upon a time, there was a trader whose shop was in the high-brow Tejuosho market at Yaba in Lagos. She was an *Alhaja*, a female Muslim who has performed the Hajj (a religious trip to the Islamic Holy Land). She sold beverages, tin tomato puree, kitchenware, assorted vegetable oil, rice in bags, and baking flour. Alhaja had no child of her own, and she was ready to give whatever it took to remove the stigma. Though unmarried, she was visited by two well-to-do men who acted as her lovers at different appointed times.

Her problem started when one of the lovers discovered that she was sharing her love with another man. The man boasted that he would make Alhaja regret her life and, henceforth, he stopped seeing her. Shortly after the quarrel, a passing lame man stopped in front of Alhaja's big shop and stared at her. Being a generous lady, she offered him alms in the form of money, but the lame man rejected it, telling her he was not a beggar but a spiritual messenger whom the spirit had directed to remove an object her detractors had planted in her womb that made her barren. Hearing this, Alhaja burst into tears and wailed uncontrollably. They were tears of joy at the possibilities this man offered her. She ushered the man into her shop, but he refused and promised her a repeat of his call some other time. Not sure of the promises, she held on to the man, but after he convinced her that he had to go on another spiritual errand somewhere else, she let go of him. She hoped he would be back some other time, but she did not know that he had stealthily dropped an amulet under one of the tables where she usually displays some of her wares outside the shop.

At the close of business, when her shop attendants were packing the tables, they drew her attention to their find, but she was too shocked and afraid to pick it. The lame man knew this would happen, so he came back in the night and took the amulet. The following morning, Alhaja was shocked again, this time because the amulet had disappeared.

The lame man showed up again at exactly noon, and she told him of the strange appearance and disappearance of the amulet. The man smiled, brought the amulet out, and asked if that was it, and she responded in the affirmative. He told her it was a gift from the spirits, but because she did not understand and rejected it, the spirits brought it back to him so that he could personally deliver it. She was advised to keep the object under her pillow so as to ward off further attacks from her detractors.

Now it was time for the extortion that would lead to her destruction. The man directed Alhaja to an address in the outskirts of Lagos and gave her the name of whom to see and what time to see him, as well as warning her of the dangers of disclosing this to a third party.

The earlier refusal of gratification had been aimed at further enhancing the lame man's credibility. The following day, she left her shop to her attendants and drove straight to where the man directed her. She found the man she had been directed to see, and the man feigned ignorance of the whole episode but offered to commune with the spirits and ask them whether or not she had been directed to him by them.

Coming out of a small room, the man opened an encyclopedia of Alhaja's life that detailed where she lived, what she sold, who the two men in her life were, and of course the issue of barrenness and the solutions proffered by the spirits. First, the spirits asked her to bring a huge sum of money—almost half of her net worth—and the amulet under her pillow so that she could be properly identified at her next visit. The man said that he would let her know if the spirits said anything else.

Alhaja went to her bank and made a huge withdrawal. The following day, she picked up the amulet from under her pillow and returned to the man.

Brandishing the amulet, the spirits confirmed her identity; this was, she was told, the only way they would render assistance to her. She was asked to personally take the bag of money into the small inner room where the spirits were domiciled, and she did. It was after this that she was told some shocking news: to cure her supposed barrenness, she needed the semen of seven different men from seven intercourse rounds each, that is, forty-nine rounds of sex total.

Shocked, she shouted to the spiritualist, "How am I supposed to get seven men's semen without their knowledge? And if they find out, what could I possibly tell them I need it for?"

"That is the least of your problems," the spiritualist assured her. "We can always arrange sperm donors for you for a fee."

Although she was relieved, she still wondered how she—a socialite—could endure long grueling love sessions with seven strange men. She was torn between the devil and the deep blue sea. What could she do?

She proposed paying for the material if they could help her arrange for a woman to take her place. The spirits approved of her suggestion but with a warning that all her desires would go to the surrogate. No! she said. She did not want that.

She eventually succumbed to doing it herself with the help of the spiritualist, who, of course, was number one on the list of the seven paid rapists.

Alhaja's woe was the handiwork of the jealous lover who boasted that he would make her regret her life. He was so vindictive that he planned to disgrace her, deflate her ego, and render useless her pride of womanhood, and that was why he went to the fraudsters and gave them vital information about her life. They used this information against her, an undiscerning woman who was desperately looking for a way to bear a child. The ex-lover could even be a member of the gang because ordinarily it sounds clumsy for a man to avenge in such a deadly way. How did he get to know these fraudsters' mode of operation if he was not actually one of them?

She surrendered herself to those debased individuals each time they came calling for her womanhood so that she could scoop their sperm and save it in a little green bottle for the "spirits." She also paid them heavily after each act of intercourse. After completion of the sex rituals, they took the bottle from her and probably threw it away because nobody actually needed it for anything.

After about ninety days, Alhaja's enviable shop had become a ghost of what it used to be—almost completely empty. She was unable to pay her shop attendants and was even restocking on credit. She had been duped here, too, by the fraudsters who posed as spiritualists because they had lured her away from her business and given her disloyal shop attendants an opportunity to pilfer her stocks.

When she finally discovered that she was being tricked all along—the jealous ex-lover came back, asking if she was not regretting her life yet—she committed suicide.

This story was extracted and developed from the suicide note she left behind. She never again met with the lame man after the second day he came to deliver the "magnetic" amulet.

In almost all cases, informants are the life wire of scammers. Without informants they cannot operate. One should then diligently pick and choose those whom he shares his life with because he can only be sure of those he considers friends; he can never be sure how many of them take him as their friend.

CHAPTER SIX

Purchase and Sale of Bogus Products

Buying and selling is an important arm of business. In legitimate buying and selling, the seller initially goes out to buy what he wants to sell and then takes it where he wants to sell it at an amount higher than what he bought it for, thereby covering his overhead and making some profit.

I have never in my life seen a buyer being led to where to buy a legitimate product and then led to where to sell the same product by another person who has no interest whatsoever in such a business but instead does all of this only on compassionate grounds. But scammers do lead people where they can get things cheap and then take them where they can sell the same products at more than 1,000 percent profit. These scammers play on people's greed because greedy people hardly think; they leave their thinking for their greedy inner self, which always fails them and at the end, reveals them to be fools.

If someone knows where to buy cheap and sell high, what stops the fellow from doing this himself, even on a small scale because he does not have much capital? Why would he decide to give such a lucrative business away to a complete stranger he has never before met in his life? How, furthermore, would he know about where to buy and where to sell if he has not been involved in such a business in the past? If he has done it before, why is he not able to continue? How does he know that the person to whom he is giving the business has the financial strength to run it? How does he know the person will be interested? You see, to a right-thinking person, there is no end to the whys and the hows. But since we all know now that these scammers act upon information received from one's close associates, the answers to the above questions are no longer far-fetched.

It was in the evening of one day in July 1996 that a young man was led into my office, a travel agency in Ikeja, Lagos, Nigeria's commercial capital. What could I do for the young man that none of my three counter staff and a manager could do? A lot, apparently, because he had just brought a business of a sort I had never handled before. He had sixteen South Africans going to Paris en route to Johannesburg, all of them on a one-way business class travel ticket. That was staggering. Well, said the man, we could not have a meeting with the would-be passengers that evening because they had a cocktail party invitation from their high commissioner in Nigeria.

I actually believed him, and we fixed an appointment for the following morning. That was when I got to identify the latecomers among my staff because I was the first to get to the office that morning, heavy rains notwithstanding.

The man strolled in at about nine o'clock that morning, and as we were about to set out, he said, "*Egbon, e ma da mi o,*" which translates to "big brother, do not betray me." That was a big warning sign to me because this was a guy who didn't know me from Adam saying this. I had to reassure him of his own cut out of the 9 percent commission on the tickets.

He then asked me to shut my door, which I quickly acquiesced to. Next he said that the South Africans had a company of which a well-known late socialite, an Ife prince, was the chairman of the board, and he explained that they needed another Nigerian to replace him. He suggested that I might fit the shoes.

I began to take his words with a pinch of salt from that moment on, but we still went together in my car. I had a booklet of my official receipt with me to meet the people who he said were lodging in a hotel at Ajao Estate off Muritala Muhammed International Airport Road.

When we got to the hotel, he approached the front desk to make an enquiry, after which the woman dialed a room number and allowed my catcher to talk to the occupant. After, he handed the receiver back to the woman, who asked if he knew his way to the room. He answered yes, and we went straight to the room.

In the room, we met a gentleman lying on the bed in his housecoat. We exchanged pleasantries, and the catcher introduced me as his uncle. That untruthful introduction triggered an alarm in my mind;

right then and there, I knew I was the one being deceived. But the very greedy ones may not have seen this the same way I did.

The man opened a closet and reached for a voluminous file, inside which was listed the number of cars they had concluded plans to purchase, the hectares of land they needed to acquire for their factory, and so on. He stopped at a stage and turned to the catcher and asked, "You say this man is your uncle?" The latter answered in the affirmative. All along, the so-called South African was speaking with an Indian accent. I know South Africans sound heavy in their pronunciation, but neither their accent nor their intonation is similar to an Indian's. At least, I have listened to former President Nelson Mandela's speeches a number of times, and he never once sounded like this man.

All this confirmed my fears about them. At one point I broke into the long presentation he was making and reminded him about the flight tickets they wanted to purchase, which was of course what had brought me there in the first place. It was then that he dropped the file, opened another closet, and reached for a tin containing some blue chips. He said that these were the products they wanted to sell and that they would utilize the proceeds to purchase the flight tickets.

I asked what the name of this product was, and he said AP4 and gave me one tablet as a sample for prospective buyers.

"Fine, what is the use?" I asked.

"It is a petroleum raw material used in the production of plastics," he said.

Its street value was $240 per chip, but he would sell them to me at $100 per chip and insisted that I go and market it to get money to buy their tickets.

At that point I knew their game was up, so I asked if they did not entertain their business guests in South Africa. He apologized for the omission, blamed it on the cold weather, and then asked what I cared for.

It was only around half past ten, and it was a rainy morning. But I wanted to teach them a lesson, so I demanded a big bottle of stout. I just barely managed to finish it; the drink was too chilled for such a cold enclosure (the room was air-conditioned) at that hour of a heavy rainy day.

With that, I bade him good-bye with a promise to go and market the AP4. As soon as I rose to leave, however, my catcher followed me, and when we got downstairs, he offered to take me to an *alhaji* that normally buys the product at $240. I objected and told him I knew where to sell it but that he should come and see me in my office at about 2 p.m. that day. He did agree to come, but I never again set my eyes on him. I had set a trap for him should he show up at my office, but I guess he sensed danger because he never did.

A friend of mine was also lured to the same place weeks after. He demanded two chips as samples and was obliged, but surprisingly, the catcher led him to where he actually sold them at $240 each. Here, the *alhaji* assured him that he would buy any quantity he brought to him for sale. He "sold" these two and never went back there again. On his way back from the *alhaji* who "bought" the samples, the catcher kept asking him when he would be coming to buy more. He warned him that others could clear out the remaining products before he comes back if he waits too long. My friend told him he would come back in two hours because he had to go and withdraw one million naira and change it to dollars.

The trick is that once you are getting impressed by the sale of your sample at such an unimaginable price, and if you are greedy enough, you would be tempted to invest heavily. Once you go back and buy substantially from the source (the man at the hotel end of the line) and take the products to the *alhaji* who bought your sample, he will declare your new products fake. Having heard that, you would want to return them to the source, but he would have left the hotel before your arrival. It is all a set-up.

Now, who is the loser? The person who is driven to invest his life savings on a product he does not even know about for quick money.

I took my sample home and soaked it in methylated spirit, and the blue color bleached away, leaving a fine little stone like those usually found in rivers. That was all they wanted to sell me at one hundred dollars.

Greed is the name of the game. Do not get carried away. If it sounds too good, it will turn sour. You have been warned!

CHAPTER SEVEN

Local Purchase Order (LPO)

LPO For Supplies

A local purchase order (LPO) is an instrument that reputable corporate entities issue to contractors for the supply of goods. Payment for LPO by the issuing entity could be cash on delivery (COD) or after two, three, or four weeks of receipt of goods supplied, depending on the agreed terms.

Fraudsters have infiltrated all facets of Nigerian socioeconomic life. They issue LPOs and receive goods only to disappear into thin air shortly before the maturity dates of the LPOs, such that when the contractors or suppliers come for their money, the company will no longer be there.

Tens of suppliers may meet at the locked gates of premises used by the fraudsters and ask each other the extent to which he has been fooled by the swindle. Some, at the hearing of how others have invested heavily in the deals and lost so much, will thank the stars for their relatively minimal losses.

In times past, when one brandished a corporate LPO to one's bankers even without funds, the LPO was as good as executed because the bank would finance it, in some cases with a proviso that all proceeds be domiciled in the bank, and that would be enough security. In other words, the LPO used to be self-secured against loan or overdraft procured to finance its execution. Now, fraudsters issue mouthwatering LPOs to several suppliers and ask them to deliver within a set time. They give a payment date that is long enough to allow them to cart away the goods and disappear into thin air. To them, it is as simple as that. But an office, hitherto bubbling with life, suddenly becomes desolate from sending many into deep debt peonage.

The fraudsters, having escaped with their loot, either discount the goods in the open market or warehouse them somewhere else and later supply them to genuine companies under different brand names.

Businesses all over the world thrive on a certain level of trust that grows into reputation and credibility. Since the fraudsters' invasion of the Nigerian business environment, life has never been the same for honest entrepreneurs because the desired trust is no longer there. Instead, there is a widespread mutual distrust that makes genuine business transactions take longer than necessary. Everyone needs to run an independent investigation on every single business document in order to avoid being swindled. To deal in supplies through LPO, one needs to know the bankers of the client issuing the LPO and then establish whether the company is genuine and whether it has credibility. That is the only way to reduce the risk of supplying goods without getting paid.

LPO Discounting

I dealt with the risk in running supplies to scammers through the instrument of Local Purchase Order in the first part of this chapter. Now I am going to discuss issuing out LPOs to fraudsters themselves. These fraudsters only use the company's reputation to obtain loans from the bank under the pretense of using the money to execute an LPO, when in reality they are simply absconding with bank's money.

When fraudsters receive an LPO from a reputable company—the scam works best when the company is blue-chip—they go to banks to flaunt it and apply for cash backup. One of the conditions for loan approval will be a letter from the LPO-issuing company to the effect that proceeds from the LPO will be domiciled in the bank that approves their request. Having secured such a letter from the company, they take it to the bank and have their request granted. But then they divert the loan to other uses.

When, according to the terms of the LPO, it is time to pay for the goods supplied, the bank writes the company and demands payment. Meanwhile, the company itself has no idea as to what happened to their supplier, who disappeared with their LPO without supplying the required goods, despite the letter of undertaking to the supplier's bank. Now, the bank has every right to demand payment from the company that issued the LPO because, in the letter of undertaking, direct payment to the bank at maturity was pledged, and that was what really facilitated the loan in the first place.

The company, on the other hand, could not have made payment for goods not received. The letter of domiciliary of payment issued and signed by the company is as good as nothing in this case because payment for the LPO is predicated upon receipt of the goods, and unless the bank can proof that, the amount involved is as good as lost. The bank must resort to making direct demands of the company because the supplier (their customer) has disappeared and is no longer reachable.

For any bank to finance an LPO these days, the suppliers must—apart from being long-standing customers of the bank—have verifiable collateral, such as real estate.

Imagine taking an LPO of fifteen-day validity to the bank for financing. Assuming the supplier has a real estate property to pledge as security, the bank goes ahead and conducts a search at the land's registry of the state where this property is situated to authenticate the ownership of the pledged property. After confirming the ownership, the bank sends the documents to an independent real estate valuer for physical inspection to determine the state and worth of the property against the loan requested by the supplier.

For an LPO with a short validity period to go through all the aforementioned bureaucratic processes and scale through without outliving its validity would be a miracle, especially in Nigeria where such processes are frequently subjected to bureaucratic bottlenecks.

It is a pity that a country that is expected to rub shoulders with other progressive nations of the world is daily retrogressing into obscurity as a result of the get-rich-quick attitude of its fraudulent nationals, who, though few in number, do a lot of damage to the country's image.

CHAPTER EIGHT

Sale and Rent of Real Estate

Sale of Real Estate

"THIS HOUSE IS NOT FOR SALE; BEWARE OF 419"

For people living in metropolitan Lagos, the above warning is a common sight on houses. Artists have now designed templates for it. It is no longer handwritten; it now comes in a fine, neat, and stylish form, evidence of its conceptual integration into the system. Often, disputes arise following the sale of real estate property (which I will refer to in this context as "house") between co-owners—such as a husband and a wife or siblings—whose interests are registered on a deed through a deceased relative's will. This is quite understandable. But the phrase above has nothing to do with these kinds of disputes. The phrase is an indication that the property on which it is written is under threat of being sold to anonymous bidders, often without the consent of its owner(s). In this case, prospective buyers have been coming around for physical inspection of the house without the owner's consent or knowledge. On numerous occasions, people have wrongly paid for houses that did not belong to the sellers.

How could one sell a house he did not own or was contracted to sell? What type of document could such a vendor have presented to the buyer? There are cases in which fraudulent sellers actually present the true deeds of houses sold illegally. Investigations indicate insider collaboration from the state government's land registry.

Fraudsters get the full address of a house they want to sell, approach their collaborators in the state's land registry who have access to its files, and get the government's original copy of the deeds. They go out to clone these documents and return the originals to their collaborators in the land department for a fee. Having cloned the papers, which look exactly like originals, they approach their unwary buyers and seal the deal.

The legitimate owner wakes up one day to see the new "owner" ordering inhabitants to move out within a given period of time lest they be forcefully thrown out. While shouting his marching orders, the illegal landlord, sometimes in the company of armed policemen or thugs, brandishes the fake deed of conveyance from the land registry.

Illegal sale of houses does not end here. Someone's life will never be the same when the dust eventually settles. Either the illegal owner, if he is powerful and influential enough, uses the state's machinery to forcefully evict everyone, including the poor owner who has no money to claim his right, or the buyer, who probably got the house on mortgage, loses his interest and eventually ends up in a hole of debt to the mortgagee. It ends up a disastrous venture for one or the other party.

Now, where are the vendors who made the illegal sale? They will have been long gone with the money at this point.

So, wherever you see such a warning stamped on a house, know that it is not the owner's wish; they do not like it to be on their houses. It is ugly. But it is preferable to losing the entire house to fraudsters whose illegal activities continually destroy the country.

This is a very extreme case of fraud. It is worse than armed robbery because armed robbers could only dispossess one of his or her movable property, not a whole house in one fell swoop.

Having taken note of the types of houses bearing the signs "NOT FOR SALE," one might wonder who is actually interested in such houses, as many of them are old and in some cases dilapidated. What is the motivation? Such houses are sought after by banks and eateries for their branch network–expansion programs. They buy, demolish, and reconstruct the buildings to their standard and functional configurations.

The individuals involved are speculators who will buy such houses and approach the needy banks or eateries for resale. What they do is also called warehousing, that is, the buying and keeping for future sale.

In order to not be swindled when buying such a house, one needs to interact with the current occupants. They must be aware that the ownership of the house is about to change hands, and it may even be necessary to amicably negotiate their peaceful exit after the sale. That is the only way one can be sure of what he is buying; otherwise, one might as well buy a house that is not for sale!

Real Estate Rent

The fraud involved in house rent is a bit different from that involved in outright sale, but there are some similarities with regard to the aspect of anonymity.

There are many "419" estate agents, especially in our urban areas where availability of accommodation is always far short of its market demand. There are three different types of agents. First, there are the genuine ones who will honestly work for their clients and get paid only for services rendered. The second type consists of genuine but greedy agents who may receive money from four clients for a vacant apartment meant for one with the hope of getting more houses within a short time to settle the other three clients. This works out sometimes, but other times it doesn't. The last set includes those that are professional "419," that is, they do not intend to solve your accommodation problem ab initio; all they want from you is your money. I will treat the cases in the order that I enumerated them above.

Good things are not easy to come by, and so neither is genuine and honest property agents in urban cities. Some will diligently do their work, taking clients around for the inspection of genuinely vacant houses contracted to them and then letting the houses out without any fuss. If there is no vacant property on their list when a client approaches them, they will be honest and ask him to wait while they look for something, and if he cannot wait, they will let him go. These types of agents are rare and sometimes expensive.

The second set of agents, as earlier described, are genuine but greedy. They show an apartment meant for one prospective tenant to four or more clients. This is not ordinarily a bad idea because one can never know which clients will actually be interested—preferences for location and interior configuration are personal—but a situation in which agents are collecting money from four clients for an accommodation meant for only one person is callous. The greedy instinct of these agents prevents them from ever letting go of money. Such agents, in fact, are not always willing to refund money paid by the unlucky bidding tenants, even on demand. They always persuade these bidders to give them time to find them another property.

But what happens to their money? Let's say, for instance, that an agent offers a two-bedroom apartment for rent at the rate of 100,000 naira per annum (two years down payment) and tacks on 10 percent for both legal and agency fees, which adds up to a total of 240,000 naira. He collects this amount from four prospective tenants, so that he now has a total of 960,000 naira, and he refuses to refund 720,000 of it to the three unlucky ones who are unable to secure the property. The reasons he might do this are not far-fetched: (1) he is either keeping the money in his bank account to yield interest or trading with the money to make some profit before other property is ready for the three other clients, and (2) he refuses to let go the agency commission that has accrued on the money he is holding because he believes that, in a matter of time, he will settle these clients one after the other. It is a game for those with nerves. He may succeed in finding them houses if he is a genuine agent, but his greed has made him bite off more than he could chew in the first place.

The third and worst types of agents are the professional 419 who specialize in real estate rental fraud. They target multitenant buildings under construction, such as blocks of flats, shopping malls, and office complexes. They go into these buildings, introduce themselves to the owners or the site managers as agents, and familiarize themselves with everybody working on the site, including the masons and artisans.

Whether they establish a cordial relationship with the site workers is an important factor that determines whether they'll succeed. If they do not enjoy a good relationship with site workers, their prospective *mugus* looking to buy the property will not be comfortable with them. But if they do enjoy a good relationship with them, they can— when they bring *mugus* to the site—address the site workers by their names, ask after the owner or the manager, and even foot workers' lunch bills, all in order to convince their unwary clients that they are in charge. Having established this kind of familiarity, clients willingly empty their wallets because they are led to believe that these agents are not dubious at all.

Thus these agents dupe people and rake in millions of naira. At the completion of construction, when those who went through genuine agents are being handed their keys, those who have been duped will be narrating their ordeals at the nearest police station. The wise ones among them will just count their losses and move on because, in most cases, the fraudsters will have left their contact offices. If the police cannot find them at the business premises where the deals were initially sealed, there are very slim chances that these dubious agents will be arrested. The police might be able to find the fraudsters if they left behind pictures of themselves, but they're smart and careful enough to leave no trail whatsoever.

Even when these fraudsters are arrested, it serves no useful purpose to the duped because their money is still not refunded to them. They continue to pursue these cases with more and more money and time until they become frustrated and are compelled to withdraw one after the other. In many Nigerian cities, every police station knows of these cases.

The only safety valve here is to deal with licensed agents, even though they are more expensive. With them, one can be sure he is getting value for his money.

CHAPTER NINE

Use Of Other People's Property As Loan Security

We all know about the process of obtaining loans from financial institutions. Collateral security has to be surrendered by the borrower to the lending institutions, except in a few cases where the purpose of the loan will be its own security.

Let's consider, for example, the process of procuring a loan to buy a house or an automobile. After depositing the compulsory borrower's participatory contribution, which is a given percentage of the total cost, the loan will be advanced and the property becomes its own security: the bank's interest is registered on the property's insurance cover or property deeds, whatever the case may be, and until such a loan is fully paid along with its interest, the property belongs to both the borrower and the lending institution in each party's proportional contribution.

If, for example, the total cost of the asset is two million naira and the borrower has to contribute 20 percent, or four hundred thousand naira, then such a loan, when granted, will be referred to as 80 percent loan to value (80 percent LTV). This means that the bank has only lent out 80 percent of the value of the asset.

But in other cases, such as when a borrower needs a loan for a business transaction like, for example, importation, the bank will demand a collateral security of a higher monetary value than the loan. These securities could be share certificates or real estate property deeds. The purposes of having this type of security in place are very simple and understandable:

(1) The bank can be sure of recovering its money because the value of the asset pledged is higher than the loan request. In the case of default, even at a discounted rate, the bank will be home and dry after selling the asset.

(2) The bank has shifted the fear and pressure of the risk involved in this business to the borrower, who has given more than he has received by surrendering collateral to the bank, and hence the borrower will be concerned with operating the business in such a way as to avoid failure.

Using other people's property as security without the owner's consent is similar to the anonymous real estate sale earlier discussed in the last chapter.

It's all made possible by people conniving together. It was established in the last chapter how unscrupulous workers in different states' land registries connive with fraudsters to forge government documents in order to sell other people's houses without their consent. In this case, others are conniving: the bank's officials.

The fraudsters who are highly connected in the banks clone deeds of choice property deeds, take them to their cohorts in the bank along with a forged owner's consent letter for pledging the property as loan security, and obtain a huge amount of money that they share among themselves and never have to pay back. The letter of consent in this case is supposed to be written personally by the owner and directly submitted to the bank, but that is where there is no connivance. The bank is supposed to write independently for a letter of consent from the owner addressing such a letter to him through the particular property in question regardless of whether he lives there or not. The letter will eventually get to the owner, and he will respond either in the positive or the negative. But in a situation in which the loan applicant is requested to furnish the bank with an owner's consent letter, the bank is not acting with due diligence and so, should the loan turn bad, bank officials should be held responsible for the loss.

This is how the scam works. The "419" big boy, having obtained the right connections in the top echelon of a bank, usually through social clubs, gulf or polo course, goes to choice areas in either Abuja or Lagos to select upscale property with intimidating value and approaches his accomplice in the land registry for the cloning of this property's documents, just as we have seen happen in the case of anonymous sale.

Having done that, he talks to his friends at the bank, some of whom might be members of a thrift and credit committee, and applies for loan. These bank officials understand that the loan is not meant to be repaid. Before he has applied at all, they know that the money is going to be shared among them because they are all aware of the source of the security pledged against the loan.

So, having applied for the loan, they officially write to demand his security against the loan, which he will oblige them with. To further the process, they write again for a letter of consent from the owner of the property, which he will also provide. Now, this is where the bank officials really connive. You cannot ask an applicant to personally provide a sensitive third-party security instrument and claim to have observed due diligence in the processing of a high-profile facility. More than likely, if he did not have the consent of the owner, the applicant would go ahead and forge it so as to facilitate the dubious loan.

The loan becomes a done deal as soon as the fraudster presents the letter of consent because the bank boys will have tossed the property deeds earlier submitted to the department handling property search. And, of course, there seems to be no dispute about the ownership and the documents appear to be genuine, so the department will come back with its clean bill of health confirming both the genuine nature of the documents and the ownership of the property, as well as its existence.

Now that the loan has been granted, the fraudster will disburse it as earlier agreed and disappear with his share of the loot. After waiting in vain for the loan repayment, the bank will commence a foreclosure process on the property illegally pledged by the fraudster and, as part of the process, paste a lien notice on the property, which will then trigger a counter legal challenge by the true owner. The bank ends up losing this case and writing off the huge amount of money as a bad loan. This is how some banks deplete their shareholders' funds and erode their annual profits.

For a bank to approve of a third party's property as loan security, the bank should establish a direct correspondence with the owner, making sure the owner personally or by proxy other than the applicant brings the consent letter to the bank. If anything short of this is done, bank officials should be prosecuted for the resultant default of the borrower.

CHAPTER TEN

Telephone-Related Scams

There are scams that originate with telephone calls and later end with an individual meeting another at a designated place and time in order to be defrauded by him or her. Other scams originate and end with the use of short message service (SMS), with the victim having willingly volunteered important financial information to the fraudster in between.

Before the advent of Global Service for Mobile Telecommunication (GSM) in Nigeria, life was not as easy as it now is. But every coin has its two sides: both good and bad came with it. There are three major telephone-related scams that this chapter will deal with:

(1) Bogus promotions and prize awards
(2) Foreign parcel bait
(3) Gems exportation scam

Bogus Promotions and Prize Awards

From time immemorial, both service and manufacturing companies have used sales promotions that eventually lead to awards of prizes either to loyal customers or those who participate in certain competitions. This is always done to boost the company's sales and enhance its customer base.

Fraudsters, as earlier discussed, are everywhere. When it comes to bogus prize awards, this is how they operate. The fraudsters will randomly select some GSM numbers, send congratulatory messages to them through SMS, and demand a certain amount of call cards credit to enable them to give details of the prize and the venue to claim it at. The prize is always something mouthwatering, like a car or some staggering amount of money.

These types of scammers take advantage of three common traits usually prevalent in people enduring an ailing economy: poverty,

gullibility, and greed. Poverty leads to gullibility, and gullibility expos-
es the greed in someone.

Ordinarily, a person of average intelligence should realize that a
whole corporate body should not be demanding recharge cards as a
condition for the release of a high-value prize like a car or a huge sum
of money. But where poverty reigns, gullibility follows, as most victims
see such messages and demands as signs of their luck and opportuni-
ties to make millions.

Another version of this scam is for the fraudsters to ask for the
victim's bank account number and personal identification number, or
PIN code, so as to wire the prize directly to their accounts. Victims also
respond to these as a result of poverty, greed, and gullibility, only to
lose the hard-earned cash in their bank accounts.

A particular network service always sends antifraud alert messages to their customers that warn them against sending recharge
cards or releasing their financial information to fraudsters who claim
to be representing the company. This warning kills two birds with one
stone because the company protects its corporate image as well as
numerous customers' interests.

Foreign Parcel Bait

In Nigeria today, virtually everyone has a close relation, friend, or ac-
quaintance abroad.

It is always a good occasion when one receives a phone call from
a loved one abroad. It is a soothing balm to the biting economic hard-
ship. After hanging up the phone, one's dejected mood shifts and he
becomes highly elated, especially when the caller promised some
kind of benefit, such as cash or goods. This is another situation that
fraudsters are taking advantage of.

As with the prize award scam, a fraudster will randomly dial his
victim's phone number, and the caller's identification number on the
receiver's phone will either show a European or American number,
except when the number is deliberately hidden. On seeing that the
number looks foreign, the victim is already elated, hoping to hear
some good news from someone abroad. When the receiver answers

the call and intones the traditional "hello," the caller will respond by asking the receiver to guess who is calling. The receiver will try to match the voice at the other end with that of a known relation and, having guessed a name of a relation, the caller claims it and an intimate conversation begins.

But before too long, lest the receiver ask some confidential questions the caller could not answer and thereby cause him to give himself away, he cuts short the pleasantries and goes straight to business. The fraudster will give a local phone number and name to his victim, telling him the person to whom the name belongs is a friend who is presently in Nigeria from abroad for some business transactions. Having said that, he will list items like camcorders, laptops, and even plasma television sets that he had shipped through the visitor to his victim for sale. After making the sales, the fraudster says, the victim should deposit about 25 percent of the proceeds to his (the fraudster's) account. He explains that the account number will be communicated after the sales have been made.

The victim, having been told all this, will hurriedly end the call with the fraudster in order to get in touch with the message-bearer whose name and phone number have been given to him. He will call the local number, and the receiver will indeed have the name the fraudster gave him. This is when the game begins. The so-called visitor will ask the victim to meet him at a designated place and time for the delivery of goods purportedly sent to him. Having met the victim, the "visitor" will bring out a list confirming what the victim's "friend" had earlier enumerated over the phone and demand some money to pay the clearing agent because the items are still at the ports awaiting clearing.

Now, considering the enormous amount of money he thinks he will still be making after paying the clearing fee, in light of the fact that he is only paying 25 percent of the total proceeds from the sale to his friend's account, the victim will fall for this trick and immediately give the clearing fee to the visitor. Once that is accomplished, the fraudster will remove the SIM card bearing the number given to the victim from his phone and, henceforth, he will never see the visitor or hear from him again. The confused victim will call his actual friend, who he had assumed had sent him some materials. But the voice at the other end will deny both having spoken with him recently and having sent any cargo through anybody to the victim.

It may later be discovered that the fraudulent caller was actually calling from Lagos and not abroad. Modern technology allows for such deceitful manipulation of a caller's identification number on a receiver's phone.

People should not quickly jump at mouthwatering offers without first discussing them with family and friends who are more experienced. You have been warned!

Gems Exportation Scam

Gems are natural ornamental materials mined from the soil. They have different names and shapes and varied monetary value. Most gems are mined mainly to be exported and exchanged for foreign currencies.

The "419" business is like the medical profession in that it has different specializations. Fraudsters have specialists in every sphere of human endeavor.

I once had a three-day stint with "419" gems specialists about two years ago. My phone rang, and I saw a London area code on the caller's identification. I answered the call, and the caller kept asking me to guess who was calling. Right then and there, I knew fraudsters were at work. I pretended to not know he was a scammer because my aim was to waste as much airtime of his as I could. So I pretended to be cracking my brain trying to figure out who out of my friends was calling. I finally called him Tunde, and of course he claimed it immediately.

"My friend Tunde," I said, "why did you forget about your friend for the past two years? Is this your new number?"

Just as expected, the fraudster replied, "Yes, it is my present number. Disregard the former one."

Now I deliberately made the job easier for him by asking him about the camcorder he had been promising to send me for the past two years. He said the purpose for which he had called me was not business at a camcorder level but a business that would transform me into a multimillionaire. So I played along.

He said that he wanted to confirm that my phone number was still valid and that he would give me the full details of the business the following day. I pretended as if I were not sure he would call back the following day and kept telling him that I hoped he wouldn't persist in the precedent he'd established of breaking promises of calling back. He gave me his word that he would.

"Tunde" called toward the evening of the following day, and the first thing I told him was that my wife could not believe he had called me the previous day. He said he had actually offended my wife but insisted that this time around our business would commence and he would be keeping in touch. As to the business, he told me about a particular gemstone. I do not remember the name of it, but I do remember that he said it could be found in Oye-Ekiti in Ekiti state, Nigeria.

He explained that there were three Britons who would be arriving in Nigeria in a week's time and that I should arrange for their pickup and make available to them adequate police security because they were coming with a large sum of foreign currency to purchase the gems. He further told me there was an engineer in the Federal Ministry of Mines and Power who would help smuggle out exportation forms for the gems the Britons were coming to buy and that without the forms, they could not export them after procurement. So the forms were very important, he explained, and they needed an "approved" stamp on them. He said he had to get the name and telephone number of the engineer and promised to call me back again the following day, which I agreed to. He was only trying to make it look real to me and, as a *mugu*, I had to play along.

The third day Tunde called and I shouted, "*Baba Tunene*," because I had to deceive the deceiver twofold in order for him to continue building his castle in the air. After the first day, anytime he called using the London number, I always shouted "*Baba Tunene*" instead of the normal "hello," and the criminal would acknowledge it.

So the third day he explained to me that I should buy the stamped exportation forms at the rate of fifty thousand naira each from the engineer and sell them to the expected exporters at 1,400 U.S. dollars each because one stamped form was needed for each gem. I was told I should buy as many forms as I could before they arrived because the number of forms I sold to them would determine how many gems they would buy. I was told to consider that they were journeying from London to Nigeria just for the gems and to therefore make sure I bought enough forms that it would be worth their efforts. He then gave me the name and telephone number of the engineer and asked me to call him after our discussion.

I called the "engineer" and introduced myself to him. He asked how I got his number, and I disclosed to him that it was Tunde, my friend from London, who directed me to him. He gave me the necessary audience.

Having disclosed everything about the deal to him, I asked if he had told my friend that the form was being sold for fifty thousand naira, and he said yes. At that point, I appealed to him to call Tunde back and tell him that he made a mistake about the price and that the right price was seventy thousand naira. Tunde, I told him, would not give me anything out of the deal, so the extra twenty thousand naira could be shared between me and him.

I had also performed another little bit of trickery during the conversation with the engineer: I had given him the wrong name when I introduced myself. And guess what? When Tunde called me thereafter, he was addressing me by the wrong name I had given to the engineer. Tunde had previously been careful to not ask me of my name because I was supposed to be his long-standing friend.

So, he called me, addressed me by a name for the first time in three days, and pretended as if he were pissed off with the engineer who had initially given him fifty thousand naira as the cost of each form and now changed it to seventy thousand naira. But, all the same, he said I should still go ahead and look for money to buy enough forms for the expected expatriates. I promised to meet the engineer the following day with some cash to buy the forms.

My purpose in striking a deal of twenty thousand naira extra on each form was to impress them with my greedy disposition and reinforce their belief that they were catching a real *mugu*.

The following evening, Tunde called and asked if I had seen the engineer. I answered in the negative. An enraged Tunde poured vituperations on me and warned that he would divert the business to a blood brother of his if by the following day I did not perform.

At that point I asked the fraudster to swear in the name of God and tell me if Tunde was actually the name his parents christened him with when he was born. And guess what? The miscreant burst into big laughter at the other end and hung up.

Each of the three cases treated in this chapter shows the role played by greed and gullibility. If it sounds too good, it will turn sour. Do not get involved. You have been warned!

CHAPTER ELEVEN

Employment, School Admission, and Visa Scams

Persons seeking employment, school admission, or a visa are all applicants, and they are all at risk of being scammed. Because the exploding population of Nigeria has been coupled with a dwindling economy, fraudsters are busy making fortunes from these three categories of unwary applicants.

Employment Scam

There are two categories of job applicants. In the first group are persons who have no job at all, which includes those who are fresh out of school and those who have lost their jobs due to any number of reasons, ranging from downsizing to their having breached the employer's code of conduct. The other group comprises those presently employed but not satisfied with either their job or their pay. Such employees are always falsely seeking permission for days off in order to attend one employment interview or the other. Only a few of them are lucky enough to get jobs before being thrown out for their inconsistencies and absenteeism.

How do fraudsters scam employment applicants, the majority of whom are being fed, clothed, and housed by parents, guardians, or friends? Fraudsters are callous; they give no consideration to their victim's condition or plight. Their main concern is how much will go into their personal pockets.

Because of how bad the unemployment situation is in this country, desperate applicants are willing to do anything to get employed. It is only in Nigeria that I have heard of an applicant coughing up forty thousand naira to get a job.

Another factor that gives 419 the opportunity to scam job applicants is the level of corruption in Nigeria. If you are actually qualified and suitable for a job, why on earth would you have to bribe someone to get it? But so many graduates in this country bought their ways through school, and they will always prefer going through people to get jobs because they cannot defend their certificates.

Fraudsters advertise on the Web and give out bank account numbers to which applicants are told to pay a certain amount of money, which they describe as covering administrative charges or expenses. Once the account is fat enough, the fraudsters withdraw and bolt away.

There was recently a celebrated case involving thirteen million naira.

The fraudster in this case was an airline employee before she got the bright idea to abandon her employment and take to the fast lane to fortune. She ran an advertisement demanding applicants' curricula vitae so that they could be considered for various positions in a foreign airline making inroads into the nation's airspace. When the applicants responded, she slammed them with bills for forty thousand naira each, purportedly for original copies of their international passports because they were told they would take their induction courses abroad. They responded in droves and paid the sum to her bank account. At the end of the day, she netted over thirteen million naira—before being arrested when some recalcitrant applicants, after waiting in vain, blew the whistle on her.

There were six pregnant applicants who, on the advice of the fraudster, sacrificed their fetuses on the altar of some plum job that was never there in the first place. Some applications and fees were even rejected by the fraudster just to make those in doubt believe. They all know better today.

Employment generally means that one is engaged in a daily, weekly, or monthly occupational routine for monetary compensation. A situation in which applicants have to prepay their prospective employers to get a job should never be perceived as genuine.

School Admission Scam

A school admission scam is similar in nature to the scam discussed above. The difference is that while legitimate employers never request money from someone prior to his or her employment, schools do tend to collect school fees and other levies from students prior to admitting them. So, it is not really out of place that a student should be paying a school; however, a situation in which prospective students are making unofficial payments to individuals or groups of people other than the school authorities is a scam and should not be encouraged.

If one is qualified and meets the prerequisites of the school's board, there is no need to make an illegal payment before receiving a letter of admission. Corruption starts from there. Stop it now before you are duped.

Visa Scam

There are only a few scams that occur without a little bit of residual corruption or a dubious motive on the part of the victim.

To apply for a visa, an educated person knows that he will have to establish either a physical or online relationship with the embassy whose visa he is seeking. When one gives out his international passport and money to another for visa procurement, he will almost certainly run into corruption.

Visa scammers take advantage of those who seek greener pastures and who sometimes dispose of real estate property only to leave the country for a destination they have never been to. These people decide to go to these new places based only on information they have gathered from others who have been there.

Visa scammers are among some of the most notorious Nigerians when it comes to documentation falsification. They obtain a huge amount of money from their victims, falsify all documents required just to convince their victims of their efforts thereby justifying their huge pay only to turn around and forge the visa at the end of the day.

A frequent visitor to our international airports will bear witness to this. There is hardly a departure flight without at least one arrest on charges of visa forgery.

You can hardly procure a visa without personally visiting the embassy, except in a few cases. If you are applying for a visa, it is advisable that you personally approach the embassy, obtain their requirements, and see if you are qualified to get the visa. If you are, you can proceed to get all of your genuine documents ready for presentation to the consular at the appointed day and time. If you are not qualified going by their requirements, try to get those documents you need to get qualified, that is, through legal and genuine means. It may take some time, but be patient; and if it turns out that it is not possible to get the necessary documents, then stop the whole process. The alternative is ending up in jail.

CHAPTER TWELVE

Over-Invoicing Trap

Over-invoicing is a process where the cost of item(s) is inflated, that is, x is the actual cost of an item but y appears on the invoice or receipt, where y is greater than x and the difference between the actual x cost and the y receipt is being fraudulently pocketed by the purchaser. This scam always involves three parties: (1) the party that needs the item, (2) the party doing the purchase, and (3) the seller.

Usually an organization sends its purchasing officer out to get pro forma invoices from different vendors dealing in what they are about to purchase so as to determine the best price and quality of the items needed and thereafter make their choice as to where and which of the various qualities to purchase. But in the case of over-invoicing, all of the above due diligence process is short-circuited, and the purchasing officer only comes in with the item and a bloated receipt that isn't a true representation of the actual amount paid to the seller. Fraudsters, having studied the trend of this racket in society, took advantage and went to work.

This is a true life story of what happened some years back. Fraudsters went to a furniture manufacturing company at Mushin in Lagos metropolis and made a purchase of 350,000 naira with cash. Having paid cash, they demanded a receipt of 700,000 naira, double the amount they actually paid. All requests were granted by the sales manager, and the deal was sealed with a clause stating that another receipt that bore the actual price would equally be issued. The sales manager needed the actual receipt for his own records, so it was amicably resolved and both parties agreed on two different official receipts for a single purchase. Having armed themselves with two different original copies of the receipts issued, the fraudsters destroyed the receipt bearing the real amount paid. Then they came back the following day with bad news: they said the furniture paid for was no longer needed.

Since the furniture was still in the showroom, common sense and corporate courtesy suggested a refund should be offered. The sales manager of the furniture factory, though not happy with what had happened, had no choice but to arrange a refund for the customers. He raised a check for the amount received from them, that is, 350,000 naira, and handed it to them, but they rejected it, asking for 700,000 naira cash. Before the manager knew what was happening, they had invited the police.

The case was eventually transferred to the state police special investigation department due to its peculiar nature. The sales manager explained his side of the story and presented two different copies of receipts that had different serial numbers and different amounts but showed that the same item had been sold. The fraudsters, on their part, while brandishing the original copy of the inflated receipt, kept querying the rationale behind having two official receipts that differed only in the amount they showed the item had been sold for.

At the end of the day, the furniture company had to cough up 700,000 naira because the law of buying and selling does not allow for two different receipts to exist for a single item sold. Though the police suspected fraud on the part of the buyers, they could not establish it under the law, especially because the second original receipt showing the 350,000 naira had already been destroyed by them.

There is a good lesson here: if you think that is how it is always being done, you could be the next victim. There are three major purposes for having an official receipt: (1) to serve as evidence of a business transaction between the seller and the buyer, (2) for the sake of the seller's and the buyer's accurate bookkeeping, and (3) for taxation purposes, that is, as, evidence of income for the seller and expenditure for the buyer. So, if you use your company's official receipt for any purpose other than these above enumerated, you will be the one to bear the brunt of whatever negative result comes of it. It could even lead to jail time if a prima facie case of aiding and abetting is established.

Do not become involved in over-invoicing. It is a crime. You have been warned!

CHAPTER THIRTEEN

Human Collateral Against Fraudulent Purchase

The title of this chapter may sound very strange to readers, but it refers to a real scam.

The elementary definition of "collateral security" is something that stands as a guarantee to return something taken from somebody, where such a guarantee will be released to the presenter after he has returned what was earlier taken away. Usually it is applicable in the process of borrowing money from the bank. In this case, collateral security serves as an instrument surrendered to the bank in order to obtain a bank loan; putting up collateral security assures the bank that the loan will be repaid because the value of the security is always higher than the loan obtained.

I wrote in the introduction to this book that "419" fraudsters are grandmasters when it comes to deceit and their ingenuity is comparable to no one else's. Who else could have imagined somebody using another person as a security or guarantee against an item? That is how brilliant they can be.

I have heard of cases in which women have left innocent children in the market with traders from whom they have bought some items, promising to come back to pay but never returning. The children left behind in this way are not the women's children; in some cases, the women do not even know the children from Adam.

This is how the fraudsters operate in the market. A woman will call on a stray child of about six or seven years old to help with one of the light bags she is carrying, and the child will always oblige notwithstanding his relationship with her because it is African tradition for him to do so. She will tell the child it is only for a short distance and point to where she is going to make her fraudulent purchase; in some cases, the woman will also offer either a packet of biscuits or money to the child as an inducement.

On arriving at the destination, the fraudster will pick out some expensive items running into the thousands of naira and ask the child to wait for her while she loads the items she has bought into her car or taxicab (which is parked outside of the child's visibility).

The seller, seeing the child with the woman, would think the child is hers and allow the woman to do as she wishes, expecting to get paid when the woman comes back as long as the woman's child remains in her stall. But, after hours, the trader will raise the alarm, especially when the waiting child is agitating to leave and insisting that the woman she came with is not his mother. The police will be invited at this point, and they will take the child to the real mother along with the trader, and the truth of the child's parental claim will be established.

In other instances, the child might be coached to act out the script. In these cases, the fraudster will be acting in concert with both the child and the real mother, who will all be beneficiaries of the scam.

Years back, a police corporal was used as a collateral security at a car dealership shop along Western Avenue in Lagos. The scammer approached a nearby police station and officially requested a police escort for a business transaction that involved a lot of cash movement. Having documented the fraudster's request, the Divisional Police Officer (DPO) detailed a corporal for the job. The fraudster got to the dealership with the corporal along with two big bags purported to contain money and went for the most expensive car in the showroom.

He expressed his interest, and a deal was struck regarding the price. He left the corporal with an instruction to please take care of the "money" in the car that brought them while he gave the new car a test run. The car dealer, thinking this police orderly standing nearby had been hired by the man, ordered the release of the car key to him so that he could enjoy a test run. The key was released to him, and off he went without looking back.

After waiting in vain, the president of the automobile company ordered that the money in the two bags left in the fraudster's car be counted to ascertain his financial position if the car had been stolen. They went for the bags and, unfortunately, found only some naira notes spread around bundles of old newspapers. The corporal was held down, and the president sent for the police.

The Tricks of Financial Terrorists

When the police arrived, they found the corporal—incidentally, an officer from their station, which of course was the station of jurisdiction—and the corporal explained to them how the fraudster approached their station earlier in the day and how the DPO officially deployed him for the job.

They also found out that the car the fraudster came in was a stolen vehicle.

The saving grace for the corporal and the entire station was the fact that the DPO documented the case, collected the official fees for police emergency or short public protection services, and issued an official receipt to that effect. The loss eventually became that of the car dealer.

Some fraudsters use commercial motorbikes called "OKADA." In these cases, the striker is always the passenger who hurriedly alights from the back seat of the machine, dashes into a shop, and makes some expensive selections from the shelf. The rider will at this time be openly communicating with the striker regarding the total cost of the selections made and at the same time be busy counting out wads of naira in his hands as if he is going to give some to the striker to settle their bill. But as soon as the striker steps out of the store as if he is going to take some of the rider's money, he jumps on the machine and off they go.

This chapter makes one thing clear: do not allow someone to leave with your wares with the promise of coming back and paying for it in lieu of whatever he or she leaves behind. Insist that everyone must pay before they go or drop the items and come back for them when they're ready to pay.

CHAPTER FOURTEEN

Thrift Fraud (The Wonder Banks)

A thrift society is an organization locally established for keeping and borrowing money. A situation in which a thrift institution receives deposits from its members only to pay out mouthwatering interests at very short notice, such that the investors get their principal equivalent back within four weeks and still have the original investment intact with the institution, is worrisome.

In the early 1990s, there was a famous thrift company registered as a finance company in Port Harcourt. The company was so famous in that part of the country that a whole month's salary of a Nigerian naval formation around the region was deposited there just for a month to be paid back in full after the naval paymaster that deposited it had received almost half of the amount on the day it was deposited as interest. This is called up-front interest payment.

But when it was time for the full payment after one month, the long hands of the law had already caught up with the promoters, and the paymaster was court-martialed for illegal diversion of the force's funds.

Surprisingly, this fraud resurfaced again about two years ago with even more vibrant and attractive offers. Most of the companies involved this time were not registered. One must then wonder how they were able to operate accounts with Nigerian banks whose first requisite for the opening of a corporate account is for a company to provide evidence of registration, which must be verified with the Corporate Affairs Commission (CAC) before the account will be activated. This time, some of the companies collected as much deposit as they could and then closed shop when they had enough.

The first set of depositors is normally used as bait because their deposits and the staggering interest that comes along with them will be paid fully and quickly. Every successful investor tells his friends, neighbors, and colleagues in the office about the venture. It is this set and others that follow that will lose their investments, as they will be coming in their hundreds on a daily basis.

On the other hand, a customer having deposited an amount of money will be asked to bring a certain number of people with the same amount for deposit. The day he shows up with the amount, he gets his money back with some interests to be paid weekly for about one month, after which this investor will have completed his investment cycle and then fall out. If he wants to start another cycle, he will come up with another deposit, shop around for a group, or join an existing group until he completes another cycle; but what is certain is that, somewhere along the line, the cycle must break, leaving thousands of people out there in the cold with their investments gone.

The Central Bank of Nigeria, along with the Securities and Exchange Commission (SEC), descended heavily upon the wonder banks and the licensed banks harboring their filthy funds and put a stop to this illicit business.

Investing in illegal, high-yielding monetary trades is as risky as leaving such money on the street unattended to: the possibility of getting your money back in both these cases is very slim.

CHAPTER FIFTEEN

Petroleum Products Scam

It is not surprising to find scammers in the petroleum products business because it involves a lot of money and the process of buying and selling is slippery due to loopholes.

Buying in large quantities is always subject to the exchange of a banks' financial instrument, like a bank guarantee, from the buyer to the seller, while buyer's interest is protected by the sellers' performance bond. The process of buying and selling in large volume originates with the seller, who issues a letter of offer to the buyer. The buyer in return replies with an acceptance letter. But depending on the terms of the offer letter, the buyer might have to procure either a bank guarantee or a bank comfort letter to the seller in order for the business to proceed.

Having issued either of the two and having received a performance bond in exchange, the buyer is then allowed access to the product for both quality and quantity inspection. If the product is in the tank farm, that is, the giant oil reservoir, the buyer sends an inspector to assess the product in the tank and give a report. But if the product is at sea, the seller's captain issues a document called an Authority to Board (ATB), which allows the buyer's inspector to board the vessel on which the product is being contained, run the quality and quantity checks, and give his report to the buyer. After the quality and quantity have been confirmed, the bank guarantee becomes cash, and the buyer takes over the product.

In a normal situation, the above scenario is the beginning and end of volume deals in petroleum products. The transaction, however, does not proceed without each party exposing his financial information to the other through a document called the Sales and Purchase Agreement (SPA). Fraudsters take advantage of this aspect of the process in diverse ways to defraud people without their actually having any product to sell.

In some cases, the fraudsters send an offer letter to their victims and receive an acceptance in return. Once they receive the acceptance letter, they ask for a bank guarantee. The moment they receive the instrument, they go to their bank and discount it just as they do with LPO discounting and then, before you know it, they're gone.

Instead of using a bank guarantee, some fraudsters use a trick involving a bank draft. These fraudsters will demand a photocopy of a bank draft, asking their victims to hold on to the original while they arrange for inspection. Once the victim surrenders the photocopy, the money is as good as gone because in a matter of just a few hours, the photocopy will have been cloned and withdrawn.

At the end of the whole exercise, the victim will find out that the fraudsters have no product, but he nonetheless rests assured that his money is intact because he only gave out a photocopy of the draft. He will only learn that the money is gone when he returns the bank draft to his has already been paid.

The third trick used by fraudsters in this scam is to access a victim's bank account electronically through bank information he exchanged with them on the Sale and Purchase Agreement signed by both parties. These fraudsters sometimes collect bank comfort letters from a group of prospective buyers only to take them to their bank for the purpose of opening a letter of credit against an expected product.

Once the victim has given them the document, they keep delaying the inspection process that is supposed to follow until the victim becomes frustrated and closes the chapter. The letter of comfort cannot translate to money, so the victim doesn't worry much about it, but the fraudsters nonetheless use it to back up their importation documentations and then may not necessarily sell the product to the victim on arrival if they get a higher bidder.

CHAPTER SIXTEEN

Foreign Exchange Scam

With the advent of Western Union, MoneyGram, and similar financial companies offering money transfer services, remittance of money from abroad has been made easier and faster. Hitherto, the banks used to pay in naira using a bank's official rate to convert the funds remitted. The government made the payment process flexible by giving the individual recipients the choice to receive either in naira or in foreign currency (typically U.S. dollars).

The banks' rates are always lower than the black market rates, so most recipients prefer the black market to the banks and hence they usually receive foreign currency from a bank and then approach the black market for a higher exchange rate. The black market operators have a sustainable business mainly due to two reasons: (1) poverty and (2) the government's lackadaisical attitude toward law enforcement. Poverty sustains their business because recipients usually only receive a meager amount of money that they would like to take as much advantage of as possible in their attempt to sort out their array of financial issues. Thus, they always prefer the highest exchange rates under the sun. The government's lackadaisical attitude to law enforcement, furthermore, encourages smuggling and money-laundering. For one, the smugglers cannot approach the banks for foreign exchange due to lack of documentation for their usually large trade volume. While a smuggler or money-launderer could exchange up to half a million dollars or more in a single transaction in the black market without problems of documentation arising or anyone raising an eyebrow as to the source of the money, a bank can hardly exchange five thousand dollars without the customer's proper identification, address, and information about the source of the money. Therefore, it is primarily the smugglers and money-launderers who sustain the Nigerian foreign exchange black market.

62

There are three categories of black market operators. They are as follows:
1. The honest
2. The cheat
3. The fraud

In Nigerian terms, the honest ones could be called genuine, but I do not call them genuine because they are not licensed and so they are illegal, though I do nonetheless patronize them. They do their business in an honest way, such that customers always come back or refer others to them. They do not cheat.

The cheats deceive their customers by purporting to offer a higher rate than their honest counterparts do so as to lure unwary customers. Once they collect your hard currency, they give you less naira than the honest one will under the guise of being in a hurry. If you don't physically check your money, then you will have immediately fallen prey, but if you count it and report an inconsistency, they will pretend to make up for it by counting the difference in your presence and giving it to you. But even when you're standing right there, they will remove a considerable number of notes from the balance they are counting. Once you receive the difference, you might add it to the money already received and leave without counting a second time. When you get home and check the money again, you will discover you have lost more than you thought you wanted to gain. And these fraudsters, unfortunately, are only found on the roadside—they are highly mobile and have no permanent office where you can go back and find them.

The third type of black market operators refers to the real scammers. These scammers lure customers with mouthwatering rates like the cheats do. Once they snag their victims with the high-rate bait, they pay them the naira equivalent of their money and collect their hard currency.

With the victim now concentrated on counting the naira equivalent, they will exchange the dollar notes with fake notes and wait for the victim to conclude the counting and return the naira because he recognizes that he has not enjoyed the mouthwatering rate earlier promised. Once the naira is returned, the fraudster returns the fake dollars. The duped may now go to an honest operator, who will eventually declare his money fake. That's how people who want more lose all.

Some of the more despicable fraudsters may insist on checking a customer's dollar under mercury light in a small darkroom even before he has paid the naira equivalent. If he allows for that, the fraudster will be sure to come out of the darkroom with fake money that he has dubiously exchanged for the victim's genuine money while he was outside waiting.

If you are unsure of the environment you are in and the legitimacy of the operations occurring there, change your money at a licensed *bureau de change*. Better still, the bank will gladly convert your dollars to naira if you are content with their rate. It's better than losing everything.

If it sounds too good, it will turn sour!

CHAPTER SEVENTEEN

The Bank Fraud

A bank is an institution licensed by the government to provide financial services to the public. It is a financial superstore that offers a diverse range of products in the form of accounts (for example, savings, current, loan, and fixed accounts). The major types of accounts—under which some other subproducts fall, depending on the individual bank's chosen areas of specialization—include savings, current, loan, and fixed. Nonetheless, a customer's money must be paid regardless of the type of account he has, except in the case of loans, which the bank has the express right to grant and terminate.

Fraudsters defraud their victims mainly of money. Because the bank could be said to be the house of money, fraudsters' incursion into that institution is understandable—but unacceptable.

As banks have an array of products available to their customers, so fraudsters have their numerous ways of defrauding the institution. I will examine three of their tricks, as enumerated below:

1. Account mandate bypassing
2. Hypnotism
3. Check cloning

Account Mandate Bypassing

An account mandate is an instruction given to a bank by a customer as to how she wants her account to be operated. A mandate could come in the form of a signature authorization to make withdrawals from the customer's account or limit third-party payment without the bank's confirmation of the withdrawal from the account holder. An account mandate can be reviewed and changed by the account holder from time to time.

In most cases, there is a limit to the sum of money payable to a third party by the bank without due confirmation from the account holder. This limit, however, depends on the choice of the customer. Payment confirmation is either done via the customer writing the bank in advance to the payment instrument's presentation by the third-party payee to the bank or a telephone call from the bank to the account holder upon the third party's presentation of the instrument to the bank for payment.

The two processes mentioned above can easily be circumvented by fraudsters with forgery and impersonation, respectively.

When a victim's checkbook is stolen by a close associate, having known about the confirmation by written mandate the victim has with the bank, fraudsters forge a letter to the tune of the amount desired and forward it to the paying bank. For the bank, having received such a letter, the coast is clear for payment, provided the customer has the funds to cover the amount being requested. The process could then continue until the account is completely drained. It is therefore advisable that one should get in touch with his or her account officer at least twice a week in order to minimize the losses that could arise from this type of scam.

The other process—confirmation by telephone—is a surprisingly riskier option. This is more evidence of fraudsters making use of connivance.

When a customer is leaving a phone call mandate with the bank, it makes sense to leave a mobile phone number and not a landline. This would also be the safer option in a society devoid of these few retrogressive elements called fraudsters.

When one's checkbook or leaflet is stolen, fraudsters contact their cohorts in the company of their victim's telephone service provider and give them the victim's number.

Having received the number, the fraudsters wait for further instruction from the striker. When they are about to enter the bank to cash the check, they make a call through to their telephone service cohorts to divert all incoming calls to the victim's number to a particular number belonging to one of them. Once that is done, they approach the teller with the check and, as per custom, the teller makes a call through to the victim's mandate number left with the bank for the confirmation of (a) the name of the payee, (b) the amount on the check, and (c) the check number and date. Because incoming calls from the victim's number have been diverted, a member of the dubious gang will receive the call and confirm all.

Meanwhile, even though the victim's handset might be with him, he will not receive a single call until the illicit deal is concluded and the criminal in the phone company enables the victim to receive incoming calls again. Now, unknown to the victim, he has lost a considerable sum of money as a result of the mandate he left with his bank. The day he learns of it, hardly could he exonerate his bankers of connivance, even though it was actually some unscrupulous elements in his telephone service provider's company who connived.

The following is a life story as narrated to me by a banker. It happened in one of the new generation banks along Adeniyi Jones, Ikeja, on a Tuesday morning. A gentleman presented a check for eight hundred thousand naira to be cashed across the counter.

After checking the account to confirm the availability of funds, the teller—according to the account's mandate of confirmation of 250,000 naira and above—made a call through to the customer and got the confirmation. But while on phone, the system went down, and she was unable to pay the payee standing in front of her. She then advised the payee to have a seat and wait for the system to come back up, which was genuine.

The payee, having waited for about forty-five minutes, decided to leave for fear of being arrested, not knowing the system was really down. When the system came back on, the teller could no longer locate the payee, so she called who she thought was the account holder to report the disappearance of the payee, not knowing that this was an imposter on the phone all along. The impostor replied that the payee was a member of his staff whom he had sent to the computer village, which was also in Ikeja, to look for some hardware. He also explained that if he did not come back later that day, he would be there the following day first thing in the morning. So the teller simply kept the check and continued to do her job.

The following morning, the account holder returned to the bank, and the check was brought out to confirm the payee who did not come back the previous day. Almost at the same time, the payee strolled in and walked leisurely to the teller, who asked him to have a seat and wait. Having shown the lucky account holder the check, he wanted to raise an alarm, but the teller stopped him and invited one of the armed policemen outside to arrest the fraudulent payee where he was sitting. In the middle of the confusion, the teller dialed the customer's number to confirm with him what she had done the previous day, and the vagabond on the other end told the teller that the member of his staff who came with the check the previous day was already on his way to the bank. The teller gave the phone to the customer, who was too astounded to say a word.

The customer had to personally call the number with his other phone in order to believe what was happening. The idea of leaving a phone call mandate with banks is fast becoming obsolete in view of the daily negative research fraudsters engage in in order to destroy Nigerian society for the sake of achieving their insatiable objectives.

Hypnotism

Hypnotism is the act of casting a spell on someone so that he or she will subconsciously perform certain involuntary actions, as ordered by the hypnotist.

The use of hypnotism constitutes some of the few occasions in which fraudsters spiritually enhance their tricks. They will arm themselves with whatever materials they must use in such acts, go into the bank with huge amount of money, fill out a deposit slip, and surrender the money for counting. After stamping the slip received and collecting his own copy, the fraudster will turn around and order all of the money returned to him for one reason or another. Being under hypnosis, the teller will have no choice but to do the fraudster's wish, and the money is returned in full. It is the stamped and signed slip he will brandish in another branch of the bank the following day after being denied cash withdrawal against the false lodgment.

In all occasions in which this has happened, the banks have always had to bear the brunt because the slip is legal evidence of cash lodgment. The tellers do not always deny having received the money, and the excuse that the depositor later retrieved the cash does not always interest the bank's management, who consider the scenario in light of scientific realities.

The banks lose the money while the teller, in most cases, loses some ground if not the entire deal. The reality is that these bad guys are out there inflicting one injurious blow or another on the banking industry in particular and on society in general.

Check Cloning

Cloning refers to the production of a copy resembling an original. It is most often used to refer to the artificial method used to reproduce plants and animals, including human beings. In the financial circle, it is usually used to refer to the reproduction of financial instruments, such as checks. Check cloning, then, refers to the production of a copy (or copies) of a check that looks exactly like the original check. All a fraudster needs is a copy of a check to be able to produce as many look-alike copies as he likes. The copy can then be exchanged for goods and services or lodged in the bank.

To differentiate between cloned and genuine checks, banks run checks through some computer hardware. Wise merchants who accept check payments delay the delivery of goods until checks have cleared because, in the case of fraud, they could lose almost half the value of the goods sold.

When fraudsters steal a checkbook, they go ahead and forge the victim's signature and commence multiple withdrawals within their safety zone, that is, they do not withdraw more than would necessitate recourse to and confirmation from the account holder. These withdrawals might be spread over five or more states in order to avoid suspicion, and the fraudsters might also exploit the advantages of online banking.

There is no financial instrument fraudsters cannot forge. They forge bank guarantee and performance bonds with a bank's seal on them. They sometimes forge vehicle particulars and surrender them as collateral against mega loans. They claim to have the current models of high-performance automobiles, ranging from Mercedes-Benz and BMW to Jaguar, Range Rover, and more. By the time one sums up their worth, he will be convinced that the applicant qualifies for the loan and disburse it without knowing he is only receiving some good-for-nothing pieces of paper. It only dawns on the bank at loan maturity, when these borrowers default, and they move to recover the vehicles so pledged.

CHAPTER EIGHTEEN

Fraudsters in the Bank

As I said earlier, fraudsters are everywhere. They plant themselves into all industries existing in Nigeria.

Now fraudsters are being employed in the banks or, to put it differently, bankers are being recruited by fraudsters as accomplices to ensure insider dealings. I have heard of cases in which a bank's chief executives grant loans to ghost corporate entities. For example, the former chief executive of an old generation bank granted loans running into the billions of naira to a company named Palm Tree Nigeria Limited, which the EFCC found out was not even registered with the Corporate Affairs Commission.

I am going to deal with four common tricks used by banker-fraudsters in this chapter, which are enumerated as follows:

1. ATM card skimming
2. Key logging
3. Dry posting
4. Check cloning

ATM Card Skimming

ATM card skimming refers to the act of downloading and duplicating the information contained in the card of a legitimate owner into another card for the purpose of making fraudulent withdrawals without the owner's consent.

There was a case of a customer based overseas who had a fat current account with one of the new generation banks. His customer relations officer generated an automated teller machine (ATM) card illegally on his account and went on an ATM withdrawal spree across the nation. He started making withdrawals in Lagos and was finally caught in Abuja, where he had been transferred to.

The customer came in on his annual Christmas vacation and discovered the massive loot of his account, so the bank set up an undercover monitoring of the withdrawals. What eventually gave away the culprit was the activation of one of the leading bank's closed-circuit television (CCTV) devices attached to one of the ATMs where he usually visited when he was in need of free money. The picture thus recorded at the branch of the bank facilitated the man's arrest.

All the ATMs in the country come with a built-in CCTV, but very few of them are activated. Banks should be held responsible for failing to activate these cameras. The ATMs are supposed to have been built not only to serve as money-dispensing machines but also to act as electronic "policemen." Most Nigerian banks rob the machines of their all-important constabulary job by failing to activate the camera device attached to them. Had the bank not activated the camera in the above-described case, it may not have been able to stop the criminal, or it would have at least taken much longer for it to do so.

I have heard of cases of illegal transfers running into hundreds of millions of naira being done within banks only for these banks to cover up the scams with the unpatriotic and flimsy excuse of corporate image protection. Fraudsters in the banks steal their colleagues' passwords to perpetrate fraud under the guise of other people's accounts. Some customer relations officers cheat illiterate customers, who need help writing checks, by filling out their deposit slips and even interpreting their account balances to them.

Many banker-fraudsters also act as in-house informants for armed robbers. They are willing to cooperate with them so long as their own interest is taken into account when it comes time to distribute the loot.

Most successful bank scams are not perpetrated without serious professional insider involvement. Insiders sometimes send e-mail messages to bank customers requesting their account details, including their ATM cards' personal identification number (PIN), for a bogus systems upgrade. Many Nigerians are being duped in this manner because the message comes with a threat that their accounts will automatically become inaccessible to them and their ATM cards rendered invalid if they do not reply with all related accounts' security data. It takes a good bank concerned with protecting its customers to warn them against responding to big-time scam e-mails.

Some fraudsters install spy hardware on electronic payment terminals that downloads card users' accounts' information, including their PIN numbers. Thereafter, the cards are cloned and used alongside the legal owners'.

Fraudsters furthermore take advantage of the illiterate, who probably have trouble operating the machines. The fraudsters pretend to be helping them while they are actually memorizing the users' accounts' information to use for dubious purposes.

Do not release your account's information to anybody. It is meant for you alone. You have been warned!

Key Logging

Key logging refers to the insertion of a key logger device into user's desktop so that all of the user's confidential passwords are monitored and recorded without the user's knowledge and later downloaded by the inserter for fraudulent use.

Key logging involves three steps:

(1) Insertion of a key logger device into a user's desktop
(2) Monitoring or downloading of a user's sensitive and confidential banking transactional codes.
(3) Using the acquired information to make illegal and unauthorized transactions with the user's account.

A key logger is not randomly deployed. It is only deployed to choice account holders at a bank where the banker-fraudsters know that they can reap millions of naira without raising the account holder's suspicion. It is also frequently deployed to the desktops belonging to senior bank employees who handle sensitive financial transactions.

A key logger device may be inserted in the inside of a computer keyboard or directly into a desktop through its Universal Serial Bus (USB).

Dry Posting

Dry posting refers to the act of conjuring and posting nonexistent figures to a bank customer's account, where such postings are later reversed by the originator and credited to an account accessible to the banker-fraudster who did the posting for withdrawals.

Dry posting is always carried out by bank employees who are in charge of the posting of figures. They deliberately credit a customer's account with fictitious figures, purportedly in error, and later reverse it by debiting the customer's account. They then post the correspondent credit to the account of their choice, where they can easily access the funds for withdrawal.

A customer whose account has been wrongly credited with a figure and later had the same amount debited will typically perceive it as a common posting error that has been corrected, not knowing that his or her account has just served as a conduit for fraudulent transaction.

Check Cloning

I treated check cloning in the chapter titled "The Bank Fraud," but that was about the cloning perpetrated by fraudsters outside the banking industry. I am now going to deal with the type of cloning perpetrated by banker-fraudsters in which depositors' checks are fraudulently diverted between the lodgment counter and the clearing house.

Banker-fraudsters clone checks when a third party makes a check deposit to one's account. As soon as they receive a third-party check lodgment, they contact their cohort, who normally conveys checks from branch to clearinghouse. The messenger or dispatch rider removes this check on his way to the clearinghouse and clones it, keeping the amount, date, and signature the same but changing the name of the original payee or beneficiary to one of their partners-in-crime. Hence, the check goes into clearing with a wrong name.

The check in question will be cleared and paid by the issuer's bank but to a wrong beneficiary. The bubble always bursts when the original payee—who also happens to be the legitimate beneficiary—does not receive the credit on his account. That is when the credit will be traced to a wrong account, which in most cases, unfortunately, must be withdrawn by the fraudsters.

CHAPTER NINETEEN

The Insurance Fraud

Insurance is a financial institution, but its operations are different from those of a conventional banking institution. Insurance is a guarantee against unforeseeable future loss. The insurer sells an insurance policy to a client, who may then be referred to as an insurance policy holder or the insured. The amount of money paid to buy a policy is called a premium.

When fraudsters buy insurance policy, they either overstate the monetary value of the property being insured or buy a policy for a nonexistent property. In the business of insurance, the higher the sum insured, the more premium that has to be paid. Premium always comes as a percentage of the value of the property or sum insured. The sum insured does not in some cases directly correspond with the value of the property insured if there is no third-party interest involved. In other words, your property may be worth three million naira, so you may decide to insure it for two million naira in order to reduce the impact of the premium on your purse. But if a third-party interest is involved (for example, a bank), the property will have to be fully insured and cover the real value; should there be calamity, the bank must be in a position to recover its investment on the property.

Fraudsters will overstate the real value of property for the purpose of defrauding the insurer. For example, a vehicle that is worth 750,000 naira could be insured for 2 million naira, the high premium payable against the actual worth of the car notwithstanding, because the potential criminal sees the business as an investment that will yield its return sometime before the expiration of the policy.

Having overstated the worth of the vehicle and fully paid the premium, the fraudster will then either drive the vehicle to a neighboring country for sale with fake ownership papers or set the vehicle ablaze. In either of the above cases, the insurer suffers a heavy loss, while the fraudster enjoys his booty.

Fraudsters have several ways of dealing with the insurance institution, just like they do with the bank. In some cases, they buy a premium for a nonexistent vehicle with fake documents only to come back months later to claim the purported theft of the vehicle. This fraud is conducted with the connivance of representatives of the insurance company who will claim to have inspected the nonexistent vehicle at the time the policy was bought.

These fraudsters will buy multiple covers from different insurers for the same property, feign either theft or destruction, and approach these insurers with fake papers; the fraudsters thus illegally benefit from multiple claims on a single property. These days, however, with the advent of the insurance clearinghouse, this trick has been rendered obsolete in its entirety.

There was a particular Nigerian living in the United States who bought a life insurance policy there, came home, and went back to the U.S. with a newspaper bearing his own obituary. His family processed the claims and got paid just by delivering a copy of the daily and a fake death certificate. But this man was later arrested in another state he had relocated to. He had forgotten that he had reentered the country with the same name, and since all the trash goes into one basket in the United States, he knew better, albeit in a hard way.

There are many other ways in which fraudsters deal with the insurance industry. The situation is so bad that it is hard to get goods meant for Nigeria insured from abroad due to the rate of claims associated with such covers.

CHAPTER TWENTY

Stock Market Fraud

The stock market is where public quoted companies' shares are offered for sale and purchase. Having passed through examination and approval by the Nigerian Security and Exchange Commission (SEC), companies' shares are then sold to the public through professional stockbrokers on the floor of the Nigerian Stock Exchange (NSE).

While NSE is responsible for the due diligence and high standards of professional practice in the exchange of shares, the SEC remains the regulatory body overseeing the entire market.

Investing in stocks is a sober undertaking and so professional practitioners are necessary to broker between sellers and buyers. Having invested in a particular company's securities, the investor, at the end of the financial year, expects some dividends from the profit accruing from the company's annual business cycle and some bonus shares if possible.

A dividend is the percentage of profit due to an investor or shareholder in a ratio of investment against the total profit approved to be shared by the company, and a bonus is the number of additional free shares offered to the investor as a kind gesture. It should be noted that most of the fraudulent acts committed in the capital market are committed by the licensed professional brokers entrusted with investors' money to trade on their behalf. I will be discussing five of their dubious ways of defrauding the investing public, as enumerated below:

1. Trading in clients' stocks without his consent
2. Illegal movement of stock prices without meeting the minimum requirements
3. Diversion of investors' funds
4. Using people's shares to secure loans without their consent
5. Diversion of investors' unclaimed dividends

Trading in Clients' Stocks Without their Consent

There are investors who trust their brokers enough that they will keep their share portfolios with them. This is especially convenient for investors who are very busy, high net worth individuals or are simply outside of the country.

The purpose of this type of arrangement is to allow the easy exchange of shares, that is, to allow an investor to sell some shares and buy others despite his or her distance from home or busy schedule, whatever the case may be. Another reason to have this arrangement is for safekeeping; since some investors live outside the country, it would not be safe to move those instruments about when travelling, and trusting their brokers, they leave them to run their stocks unhindered.

Dubious brokers will sell some or even all the up-moving shares in their custody with the aim of buying back when the prices are down, thereby making some profit in a short period of time without the knowledge of their investors. Such fraudulent moves backfire when the share's price ends up continuing to climb and, in order not to lose money, they keep hoping and waiting until for a time when a repurchase will not erode the illegal profit they've already made. During this time, the investors might call for the sale of their shares, the prices of which are now higher than the prices the broker earlier sold, thus exposing the brokers' illegal deal.

On the other hand, the investor may need the certificates for loan security during the period when he's waiting to repurchase, and the bubble will then burst in this way on the broker. A company called Trade Alert has proffered a solution to that: if you subscribe to Trade Alert, each time there is a movement on your shares, you receive an SMS—and although this SMS results in a cost debited to you, it is better to pay this than lose all of your investments.

Illegal Movement of Stock Prices Without Meeting the Minimum Requirements

The illegal movement of prices without meeting the minimum requirements is another method men in the underworld use to defraud innocent people.

For a particular company's securities' price to move either up or down, there must be a minimum sale or demand for fifty thousand units of the shares. Fraudsters on the floor of the exchange dubiously move prices either upward or downward (depending on their goal) without meeting the fifty thousand minimum units. In other cases, in order to still achieve their goal, they fraudulently observe the fifty thousand minimum units by moving shares within the subsidiaries of a conglomerate investing entity. A Central Securities Clearing System (CSCS) has now been established to curb such unprofessional conduct.

This fraudulent practice does not only make and kill securities but also contributes to the volatility in the Nigerian capital market, which has caused it to lose its credibility in the eyes of both local and foreign investors. It could be effectively checked if the CSCS is awakened to its responsibilities and establishes a corruption-free regime.

Diversion of Investors' Funds

Some busy, big-time investors only issue fat checks to their brokers who in turn buy shares worth billions of naira on their behalf. In the process, some fraudsters will go ahead and illegally invest—for themselves only—some fraction of the funds, even though the investor has been assured that he would get a 100 percent value for his investment.

The broker, after about six months or more, will sell part of his own illegal fraction of the investor's fund and obtain the cash covering the investor's initial money he illegally diverted. Having done that, a bemused investor will receive a check covering some fraction of his total investment in shares with an excuse from the broker explaining that he was unable to get a 100 percent allotment of his request.

At the time of initial investment, the shares might be worth, for example, about ten naira per unit, and price per unit at the time of refund might be thirty naira. So the difference of twenty naira per unit on about half of the shares illegally bought with the investor's money has paid the whole 50 percent of the investor's initial fund made available to the broker six to nine months ago. This is simply another way so-called professional brokers fleece the investing public.

There was a case of a wealthy woman who gave about 4.5 billion naira to a first generation bank's chief executive to purchase the bank's shares when they were having a public offer. The shares were offered for N4.50 at the time the chief executive received the money.

He bought shares worth half of the money for the woman and diverted the other 50 percent to his own share portfolio without the lady's consent. Being a very busy, high net worth individual, the woman did not bother to demand the certificate at the time the IPO ended but was falsely assured that all her money had been invested in the bank's equity.

After nine months of the public offer, the bank's shares shot to sixteen naira.

Having sold a minute fraction of his illegally acquired shares with 50 percent of the woman's funds, the chief executive returned half of the sum initially collected from the woman about nine months prior with the excuse that he was only able to procure the shares worth 50 percent of her 4.5 billion naira investment.

The woman called in her lawyer, but, unfortunately, the time of the call coincided with when the M.D. was having a serious running battle with the rest of his codirectors on the board of the bank, so she was persuaded to let the sleeping dog lie if she did not want the man dead, in view of the other problems facing him. But suffice it to say that any idiot knew that the M.D. was being economical with the truth about what he did with that woman's money.

How safer could an investor have played, having commissioned the chief executive of a whole bank for investment decision-making? The fraud engaged in here is so sad and sickening.

Using Other People's Shares to Secure Loans Without their Consent

We are now very familiar with how some people use others' property for loan security without their consent. The only difference between this process and the process involved in the real estate scenario is in the instruments used and the professionals involved.

Unscrupulous brokers charge a percentage of the loan amount, especially for margin trading, where a loan applicant needs a security to procure a loan for a share portfolio to be managed by the same broker. This type of arrangement is for a short period—say, a maximum of six months.

The securities upon which such a loan is needed must be high-yielding, as per the professional projection of the broker, so in most cases—if things work out his way—everybody smiles to the bank after maturity, and nobody knows how it happened. But if the shares bought with the loan nosedive before their projected maturity date, then everybody in the market will know what's going on.

Diversion of Investors' Unclaimed Dividends

Diverting unclaimed dividends is just like illegally cashing a check written out in someone else's name.

Dividends are issued as checks in the names of legal beneficiaries, but when they remain unclaimed for one reason or another, fraudsters will be at hand to claim them. These fraudsters claim these checks by forging identification in the names of the legal owners and then simply walking into the bank.

They also open accounts in the banks in the names of the beneficiaries where they pay out the big checks and later clear the accounts. It is not clear if some registrars are behind this. But in some cases, an investor might have moved out of an address without notifying the registrar. When such dividends get to the old address—if there is a fraudster living there—the money will be irrevocably gone because the fraudster will forge documents in that name and claim the money.

Sometimes the amount involved may run into the tens of millions of naira, and the fraudsters will channel them through the clearing process and ultimately cash the money. It becomes easy when they are sure the owners are dead. The nation's death registration database has no link to the online banking system. In other words, a dead person can still be running his bank account from the grave.

To prevent such fraudulent brokers' antics, one needs to get registered with the Central Securities and Clearing System (CSCS). In addition, subscribing to Trade Alert would be a good idea. But, most importantly, one should not leave his investment completely in the hands of his brokers unchecked. That could be very tempting to the broker!

PART TWO
THE FOREIGN DIMENSION

CHAPTER TWENTY-ONE

Internet Fraud

The name rings like a bell in the ears of every Nigerian because the phenomenon has become a household issue and is fast acquiring a notoriety of its own. It has eaten so deep into the society's fabric that kids under ten years of age can explain its process in detail, while millions of people—including foreigners—fall prey to it. The practitioners are called "Yahoo boys," a name derived from the popular e-mail provider Yahoo! This is because its operation process involves the use of an e-mail account and, of course, the Internet, and Yahoo! is perhaps the most popular Internet provider in Nigeria.

Every boom comes with its doom, and this is no different in the realm of information technology (IT). In the past—up till about the 90s—nothing was heard about the Internet fraud that has become so rampant today. It is the fastest-growing global scam—indeed, a global scourge.

The increase of knowledge of how to use a computer and various developments in the information technology world, including networking, has led invariably to the menace of Internet scamming we are witnessing today. This is the only type of fraud that cuts across all ages and genders: it involves old, young, men, and women alike. All it takes for someone to perpetrate this fraud or become one of its victims is to have access to the Internet.

Under this very broad type of fraud, there are three that stand out the most. These are as follows:

1. Dating Fraud
2. Purchase scam
3. Check scam

Dating Fraud
If there is anything in the world one might lack and truly yearn for, it is love. It is that feeling or expression of emotion that everybody wants

to have. This is, obviously, not a bad thing. An online dating tool, furthermore, that single and divorced people can use to meet partners, or "matches," as they are commonly called, and start relationships can be useful.

However, the Yahoo boys are taking undue advantage of this tool and turning it into moneymaking machinery. Considering this, it is advisable that people should think before falling in love with a complete stranger over the Internet; it could very well be a scam.

It starts with the fake registration of a personality, a totally different name, age, sometimes sex, residence, and socioeconomic status. Usually there are two main types of personalities created by fraudsters: the boy looking for an older woman, preferably a widow, and the pretty girl looking for help and true love.

Let's consider an example of a fraudster who fakes a boy personality. After he has successfully registered with the dating outfit online, he then begins the search for his prey. He sends the same type of personal data to all the women on the site who fall within his chosen category, that is, older women. He sometimes gets very lucky and receives as much as a 10 percent response, depending on how attractive his fake profile is. He then proceeds to make friends with his potential prey. He will eventually express his feelings for the needy woman and how he wants to spend the rest of his life making her happy.

This does not happen as immediately as it sounds; it could take as long as two months or more to get to the stage of extortion. Some strike early, and others strike late. The important thing to know is that they will eventually strike.

The woman, on falling for the fraudster's advances, will ask what it will take to bring the two parties together as husband and wife. The fraudster will then suggest that she come to meet him but will later change the plan as a result of some unfavorable local condition, such as weather, infrastructure, or security. He will then volunteer to meet his victim in her home country.

The moment she gullibly agrees, the extortion begins.

The extortion starts with the fraudster explaining that he needs to procure an international passport, a visa, and sundry other travel necessities of outrageous costs that run into the tens of thousands of dollars, and he will request money for these purposes from the victim. The victim will make one remittance after another, giving in to all of the fraudster's demands out of the hope of getting to meet with her newfound love at the end of the process. But as soon as the fraudster is through with his extortion, he blocks all means of communication between the parties and completely deserts the poor widow who was looking forward to a new world of romance and comfort in the sunset of her life.

The Purchase Scam

The purchase scam is in most cases the product of carelessness on the part of one or two people out of about one thousand innocent victims.

When fraudsters take possession of a victim's credit card, either through theft or because the victim lost it himself, thousands of other credit card holders' data could be extracted through the use of some software. The extracted credit card details are subsequently used to purchase items like clothing, cars, jewelries, and other frivolous materials.

Some transactions fail, though only when there is early fraud detection. Those transactions that sail through end up getting commodities onto scammers' shelves for use or sale. So, if you get careless with your credit card, and it gets stolen, remember that you are not only jeopardizing your personal financial means but also the means of thousands of other subscribers to your credit-facilitating institution.

The Check Scam

The check scam is the same scam as check cloning, as earlier described. Fraudsters get foreign checks and clone them for illegal purchases abroad.

Having cloned the foreign checks, they establish contacts with car dealers, office equipment outlets, and electronics shops in Europe, America, and Asia. Once they've done that, they express their interest in whatever they want to fraudulently acquire through cloned checks and then mail the checks to their victims in exchange for the items.

They deliberately overstate the fake checks, and the vendors, upon receipt, call them to point out the error. The fraudsters then feign ignorance but express their appreciation of the vendors' honesty and then instruct the vendors to wire the excess to a designated account and ship the items purchased.

Having gone through all that, the checks will be returned unpaid because they were not real but cloned. The items so purchased will be routed through a neighboring country, where their stolen goods will be warehoused. The fraudsters use neighboring countries as warehouses to avoid being traced or directly linked to illegal foreign purchases.

The overpayment deliberately stated on the fake check is meant for customs clearing having withdrawn it immediately it hits the designated account given to the foreign vendors.

CHAPTER TWENTY-TWO

Unregistered NGOs Soliciting Foreign Grants

All nongovernmental organizations (NGOs) are known to be nonprofit undertakings. As nonprofits, they sustain their activities by soliciting grants from individuals, groups, corporate bodies, and governments.

To legitimately own and operate an NGO, one needs to get the organization registered with the government. NGOs do not pay taxes and so they must be prepared to surrender their books (accounting records) to the government for scrutiny at any time the government calls.

The 419 way of doing business is to infiltrate different lines of business, study the operational procedures, and get involved. This erodes the credibility those in the practice hitherto enjoyed. The fraudsters come into the business to capitalize on what they see as loopholes, even though these really constitute room that the genuine practitioners of the system have left for trust.

Fraudsters open illegal websites and insert some mind-boggling pictures that appeal to browsers' sentiments and emotions so that they will send donations to the designated accounts. The pictures they parade on the sites have nothing to do with them; they simply sought out and even bought some of the pictures.

They do not stop at that. They write reputable foreign donors, often with references to their fraudulent websites, and make these donors part with their hard-earned dollars only to take the money and spend it on posh cars, chieftaincy titles, and other mundane things.

Some donations are even registered. These registered but diverted donations take advantage of the government's unwillingness to enforce laws of accountability in Nigeria. For instance, all registered NGOs are supposed to annually render their income and expenditure accounts to the government. There was a celebrated case of an NGO seeking relief and praying to the courts to declare that the government had no right to look into its books because it was a private organization. This NGO got it all wrong. If you are receiving money from others who are using donations given to your NGO as a tax-deductible item, then the government must know how you spend the money because the money makes up part of the tax due from the donor to the government. Invariably, then, it is the government's money that is sustaining your NGO, and as a result, the government has every right to know where you put the money. Foreign donors should always do this through their embassies. That is part of the reason they're here in the first place.

CHAPTER TWENTY-THREE

Unsolicited Payment For Contract

A contract is said to be a legal agreement between two parties for a job to be performed or services to be rendered, where one party is the client and the other party the contractor.

Contracts could be entered into without both parties necessarily meeting physically, as was once always required, due to advancements in electronic communication systems, as long as they both agree on the terms and conditions of the contract.

Fraudsters specializing in international scams will roll out letters to inform their prospective victims of their readiness to pay for contracts purportedly executed by the prospective victim(s). The letters disclose a contract number and all other necessary information to make the offer appear genuine. If an honest person chooses to respond to this at all, it should only be to tell the fraudster that he or she did not execute any contract in Nigeria. Even better, however, would be for them to report this to the authorities.

But greedy victims of this scam always take it to be a genuine mistake on the part of the Nigerian government and choose to take full advantage of the "error" to reap from where they did not sow. Their thinking is based on the mind-set that Africa is a jungle of a continent where anything goes.

Once a victim responds to the bait, the fraudsters will start to make their usual demands until the victim runs out of money and they close his chapter. To alert the authorities to such a case now will be very difficult in light of the questions the authorities will ask, which will reveal the victim's initial dubious motive. In other words, 90 percent of successful scams used against foreigners are not brought into the open because it would mean the victim would have to reveal his or her initial dubious motive as well as the incriminating correspondences exchanged between both parties, that is, between the fraudsters and the victim when he or she thought the going was good.

This book is meant to serve as an eye-opener and a guide for potential future victims. Having read through it, one could hardly fall prey to the conmen, regardless of which way they come.

Juicy Contract Scam

Fraudsters don't always perform the above-described type of scam by only alluding to nonexistent contracts; sometimes, they actually forge contract papers in order to deceive their victims.

Below is a story of how the president of a South American bank emptied the till of his financial institution and doled out over two hundred million dollars in pursuance of a nonexistent Olympic stadium contract in Abuja, Nigeria.

The bank director was approached with fake contract papers, and he jumped at it because greed won over the better part of him. He did not inform the board about the loan he was granting because he was convinced that the contract would not take long to put in motion and was also promised a mouthwatering reward.

He started making payments as they demanded and continued to do so until he could no longer afford further payment. He had let the bank's vault dry up. So, he decided to visit his business partners in Nigeria to evaluate the progress of their Olympic stadium. He had been sure the contract would change his life for good but then found out that the people he was dealing with all along were not real—they were all frauds.

He reported the case to the Economic and Other Financial Crimes Commission (EFCC), and the antifraud agency swung into action.

The Nigerian dramatis personae in the scam were all arrested, tried, and jailed. They also lost some of the property they'd acquired with the money. Nonetheless, the over two hundred million dollars could not be totally recovered because part of it had been lavished on exotic drinks and other frivolities.

The bank director also lost some ground in terms of his job and integrity. If he had tabled the issue at the board, the board would have approached the matter in a more diligent way by contacting their embassy in the country to investigate whether the contract was genuine and arranging a group visit to Nigeria to physically see the site of the stadium before advancing the enormous amount of money. But greed beclouded his reasoning, and he only knows better today.

However, fraudsters do sometimes invite their victims to the country for contract-signing ceremonies. Once their victims get here, they pick them up at the airport and hold them hostage somewhere, thereby forcing them to make calls to either their relatives or companies overseas to transfer huge amounts of money to a designated account (usually in Asia). The received funds are, upon arrival into the account, immediately withdrawn.

After a satisfying sum has been transferred to these fraudsters' accounts, their victims are released and taken back to the airport for their trip back home, without their ever having signed any contract but with their certainly having suffered heavy losses materially and emotionally. Some of these victims are reported to develop an in-flight cardiac ailment or mild mental disorder on their return trips as a result of the traumatic stress they suffered in captivity and their irrecoverable financial losses.

The lesson here is that whatever move you want to make, take the time to contact your embassy in Nigeria before doing it. You have been warned!

CHAPTER TWENTY-FOUR

Money-Laundering Bait

The world over, money-laundering is an illegal act that constitutes a crime. It is a process by which illegal income made from illicit trades is brought into a country's financial system in order to legitimize it. This illegal act is synonymous with 419 crime.

But because greed is the name of the game, international 419 send out bait letters that claim there is a huge amount of stolen dollars that needs to be laundered. Greedy foreigners will fall for this because of the mouthwatering reward deceitfully offered by the fraudsters.

Fraudsters pick up their foreign telephone directory, which they are willing to buy at a very high price because it is the major tool they use to operate across national boundaries.

They send out thousands of fax messages to different numbers, relying on probability to result in some responses. Out of about one hundred letters, a single response is all they need, because for somebody to respond to laundering money-laundering propositions shows that there is a high degree of greed and some disposition toward crime in him. The letter—which always betrays the writer's poor grasp of the English language—could state, for instance, that the writer is a top official in the Foreign Exchange Department of the Central Bank and has intercepted some money meant to be transferred to the Nigerian government in the country where the victim is a resident. It might then promise that a quarter of the total sum will be ceded to the victim if he is willing to volunteer his personal account for use as a conduit for the transaction.

Once the victim responds, it shows that he is interested, and since he is interested, the questions he will be asking will simply deal with how to smooth out the rough edges of the deal, and before long he will forward his bank account number and other useful information. With these pieces of information, the fraudsters will electronically break into the victim's account and clear whatever balance it has.

During correspondence, the fraudsters may advise the victim to shore up his account balance to the tune of, say, five hundred thousand dollars or more so that when an amount of twenty million dollars hits the account, the system will not raise an alarm. With this type of advice, the victim may sell his house and then call some friends to jointly invest in the deal if he still does not have enough to meet the fraudsters' minimum bank balance requirement. Unknown to him, of course, they are only asking for more money to steal from his account.

On the other hand, when the victim is hooked, they might start demanding advance fees to settle certain people who are in the know of the deal, and then they might tack on telegraphic, administrative, and other nonexistent charges that could amount to a reasonable proportion of the expected twenty million dollars.

Having paid all these charges, the victim will be asked to pay for a one-way ticket for a family of eight or more through wire transfer or Western Union. The money supposedly being paid for the airfare is actually for the bank officials privy to the deal because as soon as the illegal transfer goes through to the victim's account, he has to immediately proceed to the victim's country along with his family to avoid being caught and prosecuted in Nigeria.

What legal or moral justification would the victim have to report his ordeal to the authorities after being so duped? There are millions of similar cases that victims do not report because they would not be able to present their criminal correspondences to the authorities that could help them.

Crime is crime anywhere in the world. It does not matter which country it originates from. If it sounds too good, it will turn sour. Do not get involved!

CHAPTER TWENTY-FIVE

False Will

A will is a document issued or written by a person that states how her property and institutions, as the case may be, should be distributed among her loved ones when she is no more.

The process of distribution of a person's property is called will execution, and the person in charge of the distribution is called either the will administrator or the will executor. The content and quality of a will depends on the amount of wealth the deceased acquired during his or her lifetime.

International fraudsters, in the preliminary stages of their scams, often use a will as bait for their foreign victims. Since their scams are international, they use an electronic medium to communicate their requests to their prospective victims, as in the case of money-laundering. Sometimes they also send letters by post to their victims.

The fraudster will typically introduce himself as a son of a prominent and wealthy African figure who has just died and left behind a whopping amount—say, forty million dollars. It is actually not out of place for a wealthy father to leave behind such an estate for a child, but this fraudster will claim that his peculiar situation has prompted him to seek protection from a reliable individual abroad.

The fraudster will tell his victim that his mother was not officially married to his dead father and that the children of his father's legal wife are envious of what their father left for him, such that his life is no longer safe in Nigeria. So, he will say, he is looking for a very honest person who will not betray him after transferring his inheritance to his or her foreign account. In this type of scenario, there are two reasons why a victim might fall prey: greed or compassion. Having responded to the fraudster's request, the victim's interest is registered, notwithstanding on what grounds the victim is interested.

Before such a huge amount of dollars can be transferred, the fraudster will insist that the vault fees where the raw dollars are being kept must be paid. After the victim pays those, the fraudster will then request payment for clearance fees, remittance fees, and tips for Central Bank officials who are in charge of the money transfer. All these charges are only fractions of the sum the victim expects to receive, so he willingly complies. Having collected all these bogus fees, the fraudster now tells his victim to beef up his current account if he is not the very rich type.

The final onslaught is the draining of the victim's account, after which the fraudster will stop all forms of communication with the victim. The honest victims who are out to help on compassionate grounds are those that report such cases to their countries' authorities, while the greedy ones do not because it would reveal their own fraudulent intent.

It is interesting that despite the widespread information available about the 419 scam, people still fall prey to the fraudsters every day. When someone compassionate is caught unawares, as sometimes happens, the best approach for him is to contact his country's embassy in Nigeria before jumping for the offer. As usual, when it sounds too good, it will turn sour. Do not get involved. You have been warned!

CHAPTER TWENTY-SIX

Foreign Donations Bait

An international donation consists of humanitarian assistance from the donor nation to the recipient country. It is common between the relatively rich Western countries and African or other third-world countries.

The gifts are usually from the Western world to the third world and not the other way around. A situation in which, for example, an American is told that a donation in the millions of dollars is coming from some part of Africa to his country is, to say the least, a hoax. I do not know of any country in Africa that is comfortable enough economically to even think of donating to a government or a nongovernmental organization (NGO) in the United States or any country in Europe for any reason whatsoever.

So, for an American to believe that an individual African has decided to donate a huge sum of money to an NGO in the United States speaks volumes about what is going on in his mind. Here is a continent that is grappling with the challenges of an extended family culture that hobbles the advancement of an average African. An African could never justify such a donation in the face of the monstrous poverty ravaging the entire continent.

My native Yoruba people describe such a ridiculous scenario as like fetching water to the ocean with a spoon. But fraudsters are very creative and know how the principles of probability work; they know that, however bizarre a proposal sounds, at least one out of one hundred will fall for it, and just one victim is all they need to get all the money they want for a whole year, depending on how buoyant the victim is.

International 419 fraudsters will send out hundreds of letters, purportedly from a wealthy barren widow who is nursing a terminal disease like cancer and wishes to donate some millions of dollars to any NGO that helps children. The fraudster will claim that he will make the prospective victim the administrator of one of these funds with his own attractive fees.

The motivation for the victim here is the mouthwatering administrator's fee, which in most cases is said to run into the millions of dollars. The scam conducted is very similar to those earlier discussed that involve wills and money-laundering, but the fraudsters in these cases take slightly different approaches.

The fraudster, claiming to be an old woman on her sickbed, will direct all correspondences to her lawyer, whose name and number is given in the first letter. The so-called lawyer is really the boss, who actually could be a legal practitioner, criminologist, or psychologist. Once the victim responds, the rest of the scam is to be finished by the professional boss. Because the originator of the scam claims to be a sick old woman, it makes sense for her lawyer to take over the telephone conversation aspect of the deal.

As earlier said, the purpose of this scam is to drain the victim financially. Having done that, the fraudster will stop picking up the victim's calls or, better still, throw away the subscriber identity module (SIM) card used for the operation, since fraudsters always use it as a dedicated line to the victim alone.

Whoever you are, if you are desirous to help in Nigeria, you should make your country's embassy the go-between. Anything short of that will result in big losses!

CHAPTER TWENTY-SEVEN

Money Order Alteration

A money order is an official instrument of payment issued by a financial institution or the post office. It is usually as good as cash, that is, upon receipt of a money order in exchange for goods or cash, such goods or cash must be released immediately. Money orders come in different denominations, as specified by the purchaser, with such denominations denoting their cash value.

Money order alteration is a simple act that requires altering the amount specified on the instrument to a higher value. This process—called "upgrading"—borders on cloning and is usually done by unscrupulous printers.

When fraudsters buy money orders abroad, they send them to their local correspondents in Nigeria for upgrading. Having received the foreign money orders, these correspondents go to work, performing the necessary upgrading and then sending the money orders back to original sender.

The fraudster goes to a post office ask for about five hundred pieces of money order in $1 denominations each. After he pays for them, they are delivered to him, and he sends them to Nigeria.

His local counterpart, upon receiving the instruments, goes to his fraudster-printer, who will alter each piece to $100 through cloning. This makes for a whopping $99 difference. Multiplied by five hundred, that comes out to a profit of $49,500 in a single transaction.

Some of the local representatives also swindle their foreign principals by diverting the upgraded instruments to other parties abroad to cash and remit their own share to them, thereby leaving the principal investor in the cold.

It is not a surprise move on the part of fraudsters; it is only natural for them to do something like this.

This book definitely cannot cover all the tricks used by global financial terrorists, but it is meant to serve as a guide for would-be victims and hence it is meant to expose fraudsters' basic operational principles to readers worldwide.

If you benefit from this book, kindly pass it on to others who for one reason or another might not be able to buy their own copies.

www.ingramcontent.com/pod-product-compliance
Lightning Source LLC
Chambersburg PA
CBHW070157290526

45789CB00002B/811